The Chrysalis Theory

A Collection of Poems and Reflections

Sade Hobson

ISBN 978-1-7348615-2-5
Library of Congress Cataloging in Publication Data
is available upon request.

Book Design by Bilal Rasheed
Book Cover Design by Sade Hobson
Printed in the United States of America.

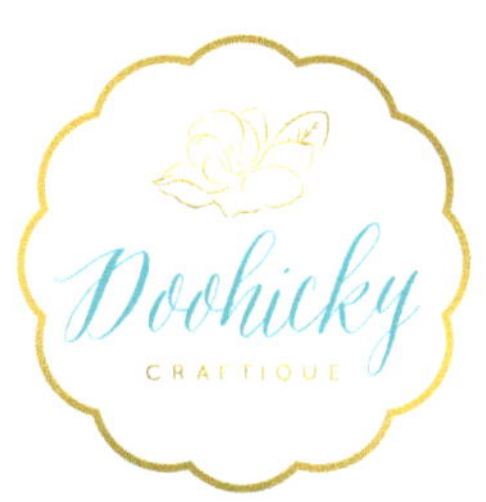

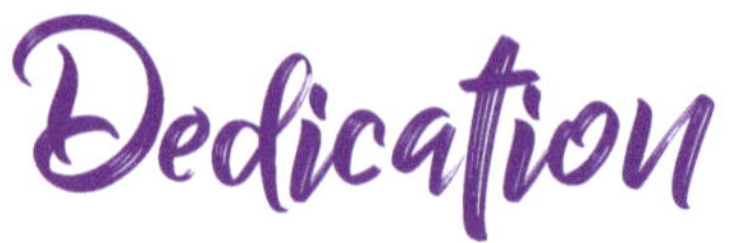

Ancestors,

Thank you for your love and continued development of my spirit. The journey isn't always easy, but the lessons are appreciated. You teach me to keep my worth high.

This book is dedicated to my soul family.
Thank you for cherishing me as I am.
I love you.

Evolution of a Butterfly

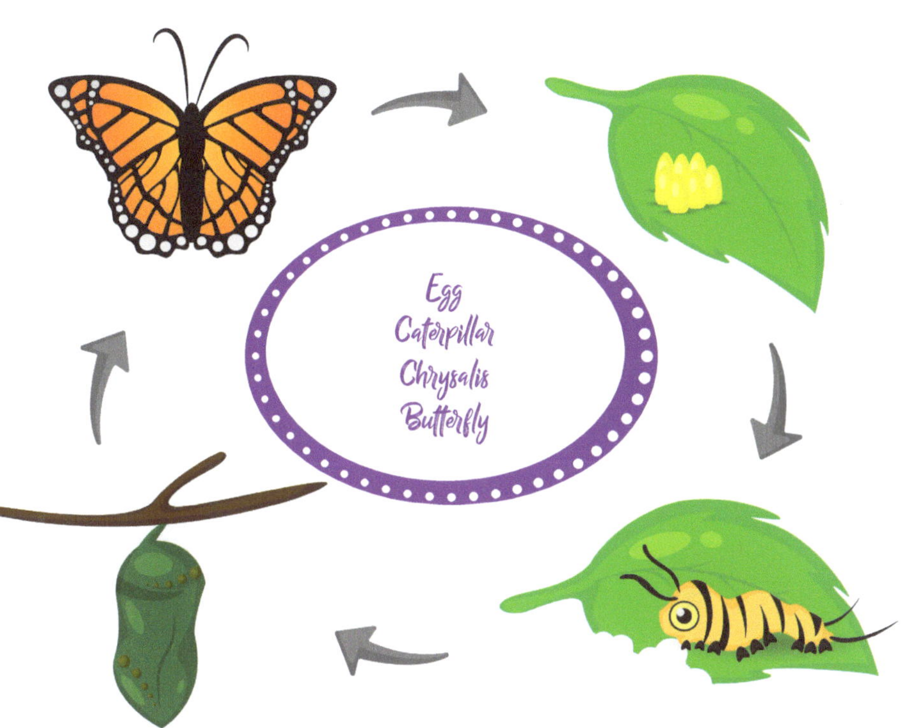

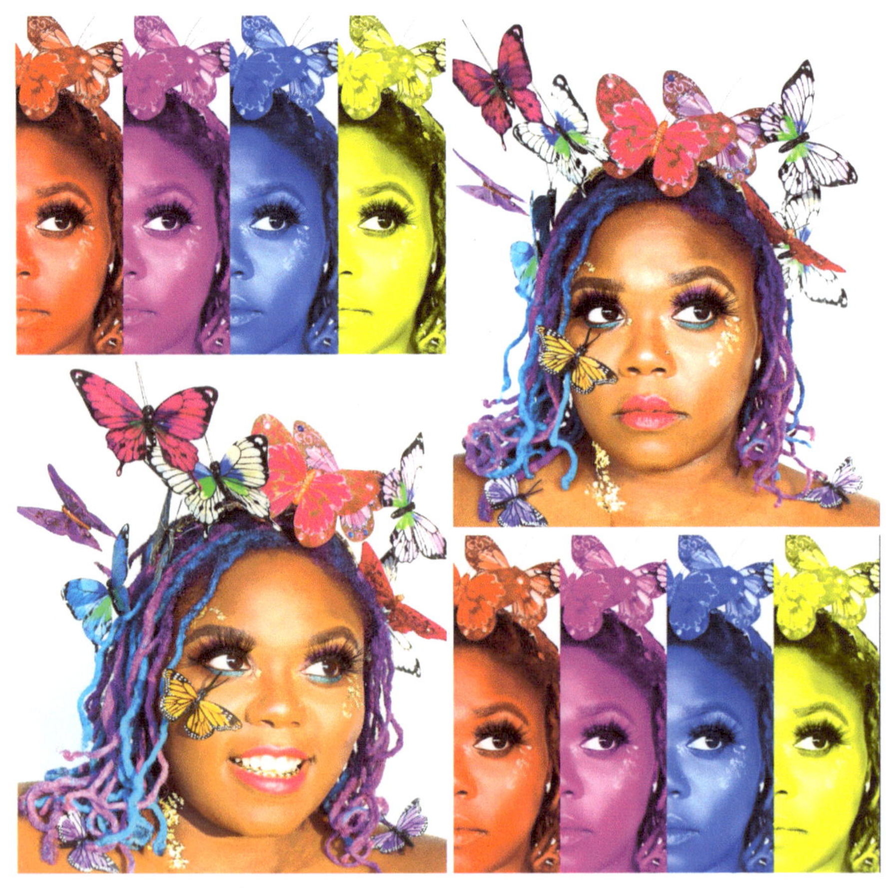

The Chrysalis Theory

2020 took me through some transformative states. A shedding of old ideas, processes and ways of maneuvering through relationships, including the one with myself. I dissolved into my own thought processes. Sometimes the very circumstances that propel, also devour. Am I better for it? Hopefully, my soul grew more beautiful, if not to you, at most to me.

Table of Contents

01

THE EGG

THE CATERPILLAR

THE CHRYSALIS

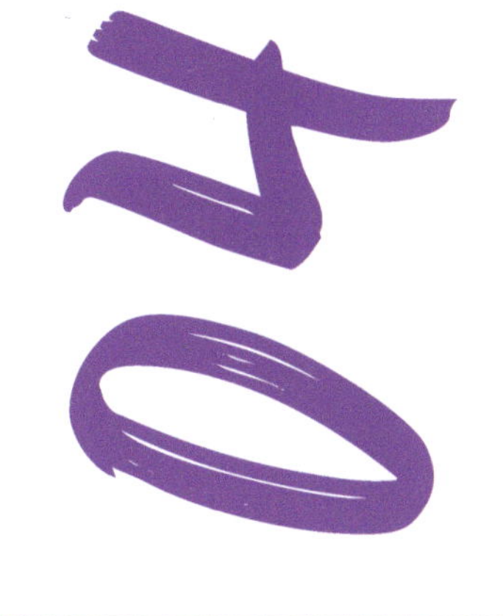

THE BUTTERFLY

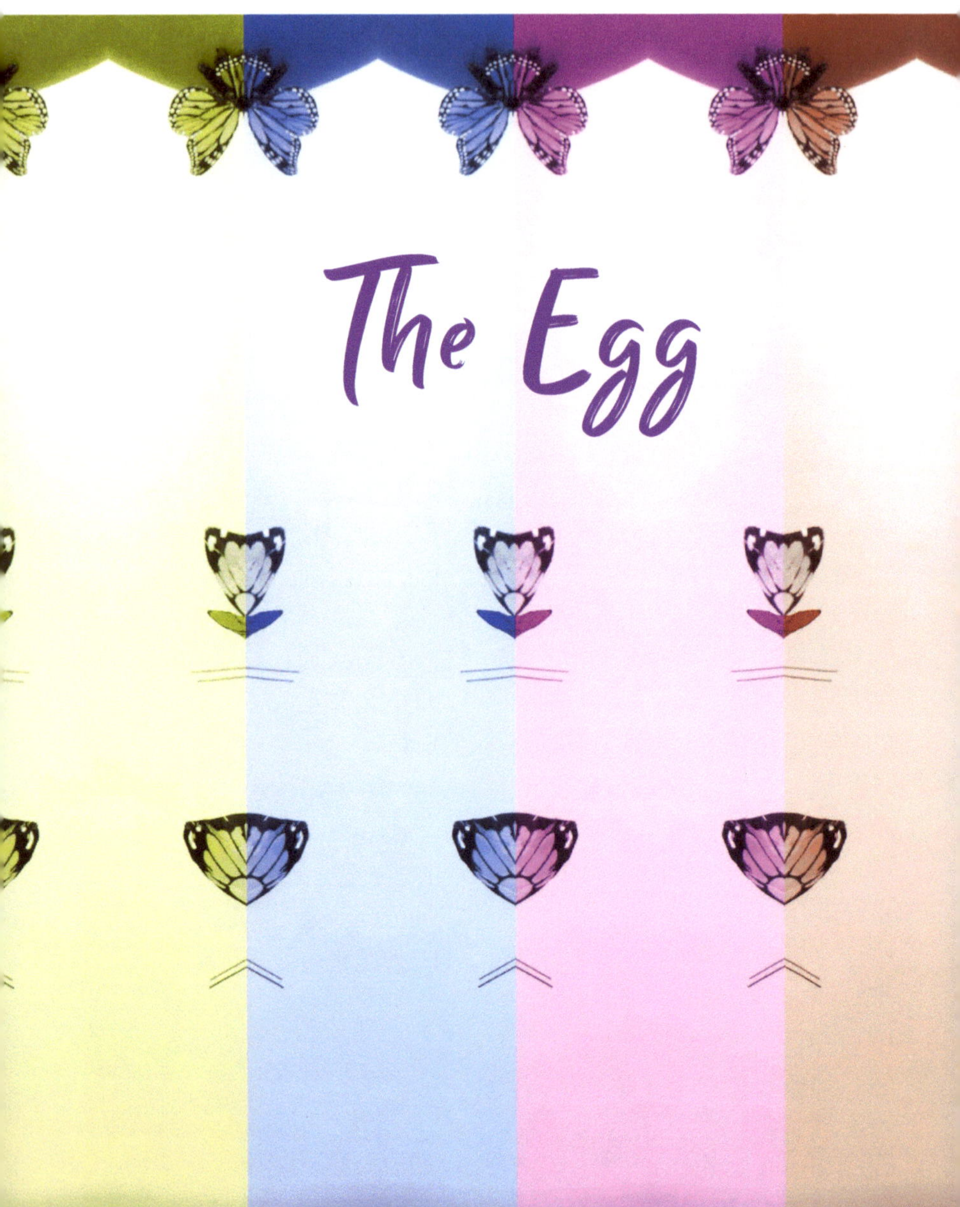
The Egg

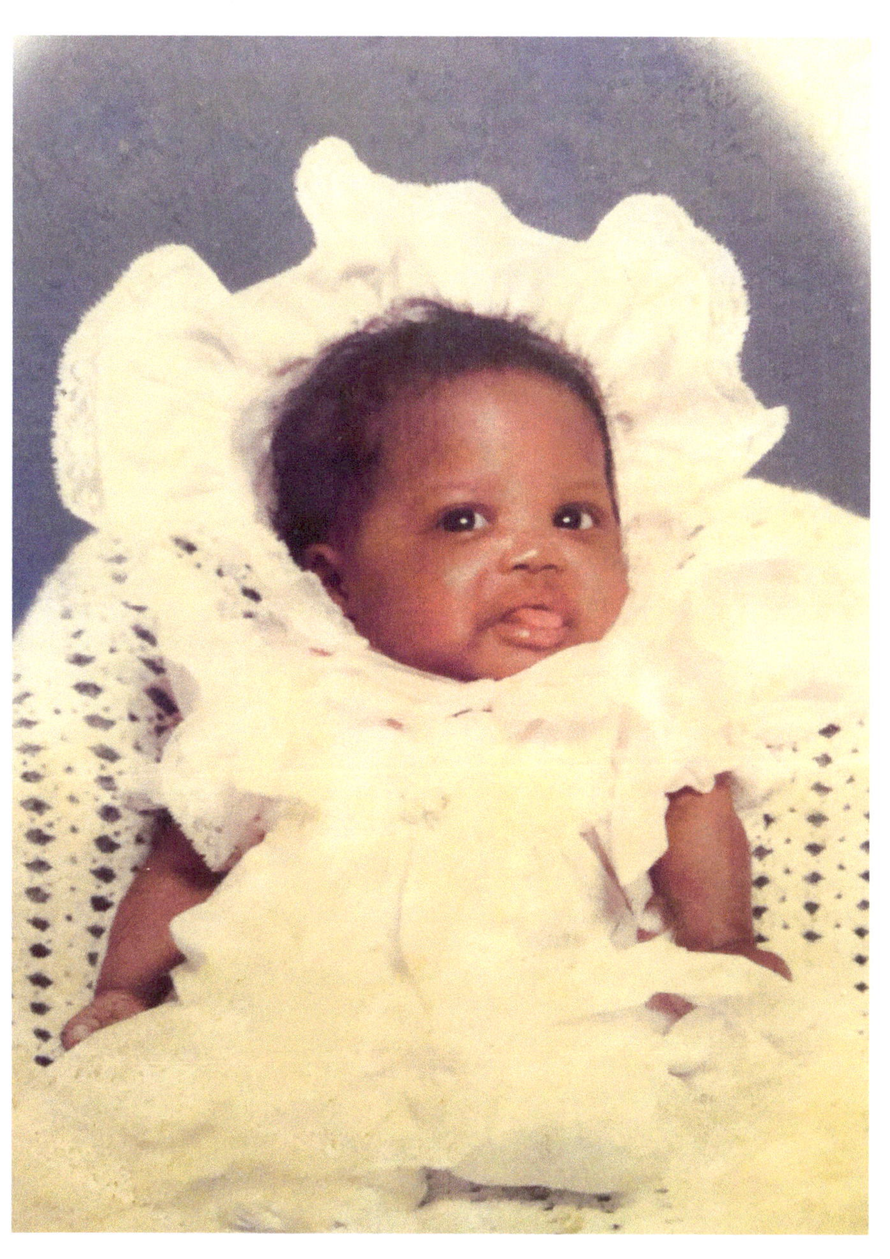

I been side eyeing these men

Healing

I am still healing. Move the fuck around.

(in the infamous words of Nicki Minaj, you can't give it to them dry like that, you got to get that shit wet first)

House of Mirrors

2020 earned the house of mirrors theme. So many people entered my life representing illusions. These interactions held me responsible for my contribution to the illusions in my life. I instantly feel if people are genuine. People react in various ways. They either become angry because they feel face their shit (this I love because it also helps me, symbiotic vs parasitic, you know?), or run because I represent an unexpected aspect of themselves, they're not ready to address. Interesting, yet slightly exhausting.

2020

2020 tricked our ass. Everyone said how 2020 was the year of perfect vision. Coronavirus, a physical symptom of how we treat each other. A display of the capitalistic sickness in the US. Wearing masks and gloves, panic overtaking the grocery store aisles. People receiving stimulus checks yelling "I'm feeling real "stimmy!" Toilet paper surprisingly the hot commodity.

2020 took us down, led into the upside down by an orange face clown. He stared this country in our face and said the Rona was nonexistent. He don't care about any life, or the blood stains spilled by his pasty hands. A system upheld by hate barraging as "Making America Great Again." America has never been great to me. A country led by old white men with fragile masculinity, hardly any better than their ancestors who swam in tea. A land of unbridled crooks.

2020 rapturing us, we've lost Kobe, Little Richard, Chadwick and my Uncle Aaron. The ancestors decided they were reclaiming their time. They came in this year like "Alright chirren, it's time to sit y'all ass down. You've forgotten who you are and we about to turn this mess around." A wrath of hurricanes, a plague, taking people who didn't get to "gracefully age". 2020 softened me. Helped me realize even more that a meeting with death could be a footstep out the door. A year full of shadow work and clarity, 2020 is still our year.

Five Finger Haiku

Intermittent teasing,

Sex upon your fingertips,

Suck me into Submission

Sirens

Sirens all through the hood, mythical beings of seduction.

Looked down upon but always ahead of the next trend.

A game of sex and they always play to win.

Strutting down walkways carrying diamonds between their thighs.

One look sparks lust in a mortal man's eyes.

Their pussies served like hor d'oeuvres.

Attitudes only palatable in bed,

Sirens ride dick so good,

niggas turning down head.

Every stroke releases a bit of insanity.

Sirens call to the part of men that just want to be free,

consuming, digesting their full cream of seduction.

Sirens so powerful but reduced to objects of fucking.

Dark feminine Haiku

Tempting succubus,

Enraged evening the score,

Fighting inner wars

Dick fishing

Verb: the act of men taking a picture of their penis in a way where objects may be smaller than they appear.

Some men act like they have a problem with angles and filters until it's time for a dick pic. Then it's dickfish city. Dick fishing is the worst. It's like getting your mouth tuned up for a steak and getting served Vienna's sausages. All pun intended. You're childish as hell if you dick fishing people. Dick-fishing translates to personality too. Out here pretending they want the sun, moon and stars when they only want some pussy. Some women into giving that type of arrangement, hell, depending on the day I might be too. Just be honest! The data gained from dating after marriage opened my eyes in the most hilariously annoying ways. Anyways, I'm creating a measurement filter specifically for dick pics, y'all don't steal my idea.

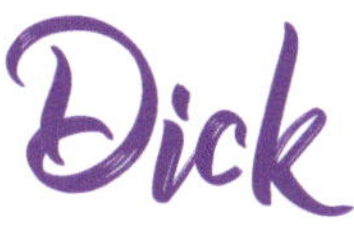

Tool of magical interjection

That rises and falls with love or lust

Careful, it's about to busssssssst.

PTDD

Post Traumatic Dick Disorder

How you give me that bomb ass, big ass, slapping ass dick and then not speak to me for weeks? Got me over here looking like freak of the week, and I don't even get down like that. Sex so good, my knees weak. Feigning and fumbling, beating my meat ain't even half as fun as it used to be. Can't even think about touching myself without visualizing you and me. Your touch has secured a forever place on my appointment list. You got a boo? Oh, tell that bitch she can come too! Dick too good to pass up, got me thinking about letting her cut! Pussy willing to do whatever, she said, if she gets you. Fucking you was like a battle between my heart, brain, and pussy, never returning the same. I should've listened to my higher self because she really be knowing. Damn, my inner heaux showing. My lower self to blame, shouting bihhhh just do it! You deserve this. One moment of bliss done woke the bear. That's wack as hell cuz I really planned on taking my talents elsewhere. Then your text came through, and pussy said, "you can stay at home, but I'm going where I'll be coming too." Pussy got ptdd, post traumatic dick disorder. Damn, what I let her do?! Pussy get triggered every time she run into you. Therapist heard about it, now she wants some too. Gahhhh damn I got to stay my ass away from you.

Dark Masculine

Wounded healer ready for war

Can't see he already has what he prayed for,

Dark masculine, loving him is a chore

Venus Retrograde

Venus Retrograde hounding my ass. I suppress my emotions of needing physical touch in efforts of not giving myself to randoms. My feelings throwing a real temper tantrum.

2 Paths to Portal

Bodies entangled. Room warmed in red light.

Lustful cornucopia of visuals, deciphering my leg,
from her leg to your head.

Three ways to heaven and two paths to portal.

Candles burning but nothing at this moment
outshines having two yonis at your command.
Salivating as we conjoin at the hips, savoring the
sweetness I left on your lips.

I inhale as you enter with the eye contact of a
sharpshooter.

As my velvet walls envelop you, passionate
whimpers escape your mouth

"you know how long I've been waiting to kiss you?"

fantasizing about sucking and fucking you into
submission.

Every stroke emanates a new rendition.

The eroticism of you pleasing another woman
invokes my inner vixen.

A voyeur's ultimate feast,

Clapping cheeks, wet kisses, alleviating your love
all over her has me smitten.

Let's not get it twisted, your eyes stay on me. Hand
coiled around my vishudda provoking intonations
of ecstasy,

decadent visions of oral fixations,

made for speaking life and swallowing yours away.

3 ways to heaven and 2 paths of portal.

Pride yields arrogance. Arrogance births illusions. And illusions inflict heart break.

Pride Rock

My love has no prerequisites, I love you for free. And even when you're running, I see you in my dreams. When you're hurting, daggers of your emotions penetrate me, and I send love to kill it. See this is more than a feeling, this amity invokes a past love and a soul healing. If you felt my heart cry out to you, then why are you appealing? The eternal infinity of God cannot be duplicated in finality. Each star and planet in the universe embody seven forms. An ethereal collaboration of magnetism, electricity, light, ether, gases, liquids, and solids; but to me they possess every essence of you. I love you on purpose, through purpose, and I swear every time you open your mouth, God speaks out. Bae, say it to me one more time, roar to me kind, open my eyes to the lessons and the blessings we experienced 12 lives ago. Gazing at your chiefin' eyes, I'm reminded of the promises our spirits made among the cosmos. That I'll keep you wild, honest, and free. And for every instance I may make you blue, that when we collide on earth's plane, I won't shatter you, but mirror everything you tried to conceal. Nurture you to mend every chip at your heart and heal. But if you don't relinquish your lion like pride, you'll soon learn why Simba's pride was just a rock. Have you ever wondered why the lion is the king of the jungle, but no jungles exist in Africa? Because the lion is displaced because of his misplaced promises that sent his Divine away. Chasing a karmic has left your heart as barren as the sky with dimly lit stars, scared to love. I can still light it up, be your moon, and drive out all your scars. I'm loving you heavily, bid to our ancestors that you remember me before we leave this astral plane. Understand your very presence can be just as dramatic as you speaking my name. It washes away any disruptions, misjudgments, insecurities in me, and raises my vibrations to heavenly spaces, as I consume your very essence. Deep throating you into ecstasy, mad at yourself cuz you didn't want it to be me. I see through you and know my heart runs to you hastily. I won't pretend. Even when I'm angry, I try my best to understand you. Despite the way you behave carnally, I know that spark of me, that lives inside of you reacts metaphysically at every hint of my name. So, trust me when I say, I love you for free, even on your worst day.

Prisms

So, you were never meant to fall in love with me but meant to be an object of my lustful obsessions. Daydreaming about your hands canvassing my body, your hand seeking the honey of my pot, finding its way into my panties erupting waterfalls of squirt.

While savoring my essence, I ask, "pussy good?" As the words, "pussy divine baby" quiver among your lips. Conciliating every fracture from those who were afraid of riding the curves.

Sovereignly owning your kinks. Damn, you are sultry, dominating, and deep. As you tighten the ropes, the distance between your mouth and my ear disappears. Playing me like strings on your favorite guitar, harmonies emerge from various parts of my body, imitating sound bowls of my divine self, aligning every chakra, heightening shakti.

So, I never meant to fall in love with you. Perpetuating true freedom allowed our love to multiply by three. Tricked me into believing you held space for me. They are right to call you the great destroyer. Invading my thoughts, convincing myself your heart reflects my light. Shame on me for accepting skewed visions of lust, quenching the sweetness missing from your life.

Realization

A connection of premature endings infiltrated by arrogance. Vagueness fills each conversation. Suggesting a level of ownership but no insight of an outcome. Words rang of too many women in your energy. Issuing red flags like warning tickets. Treating your heart like there is a cost of admission.

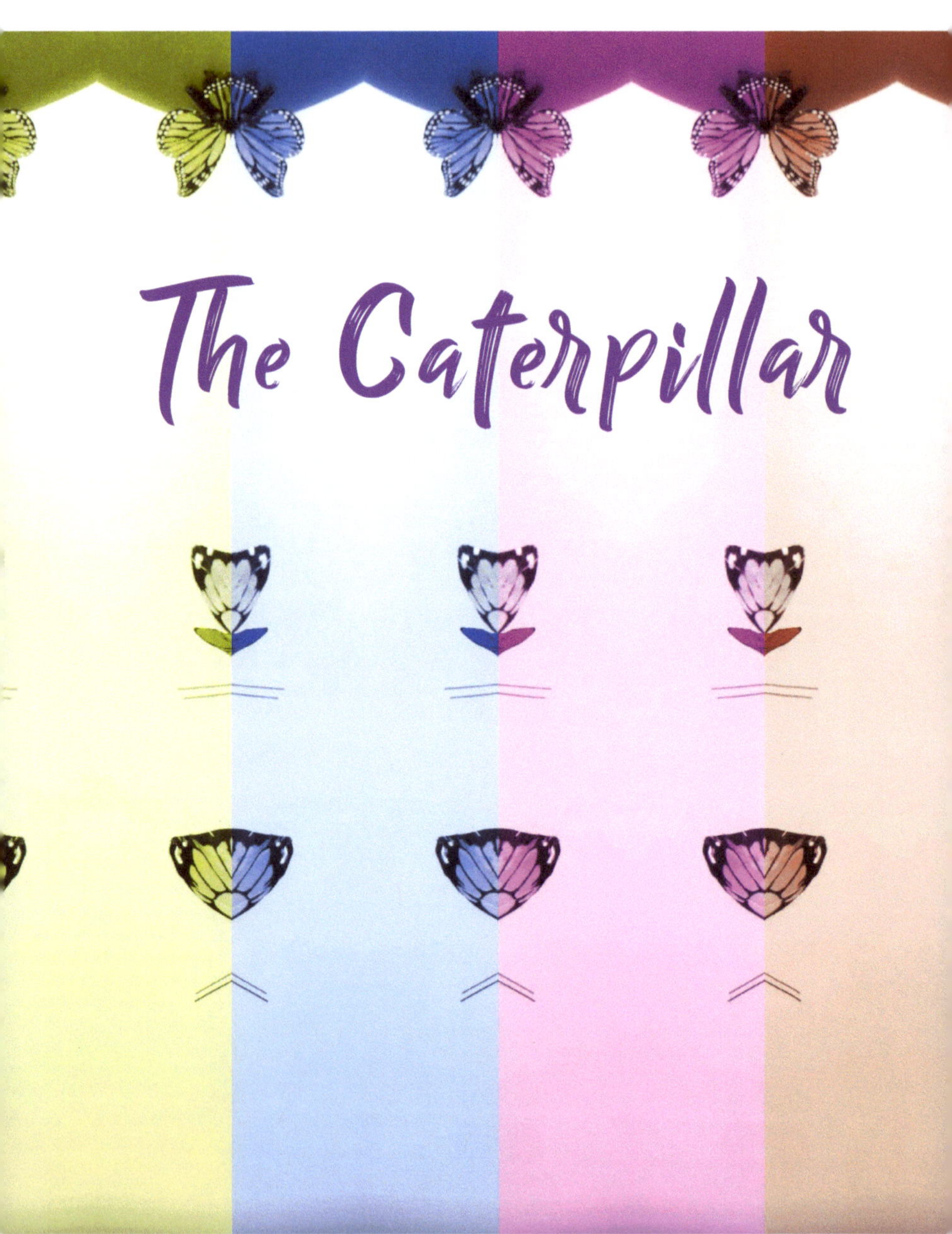

The Caterpillar

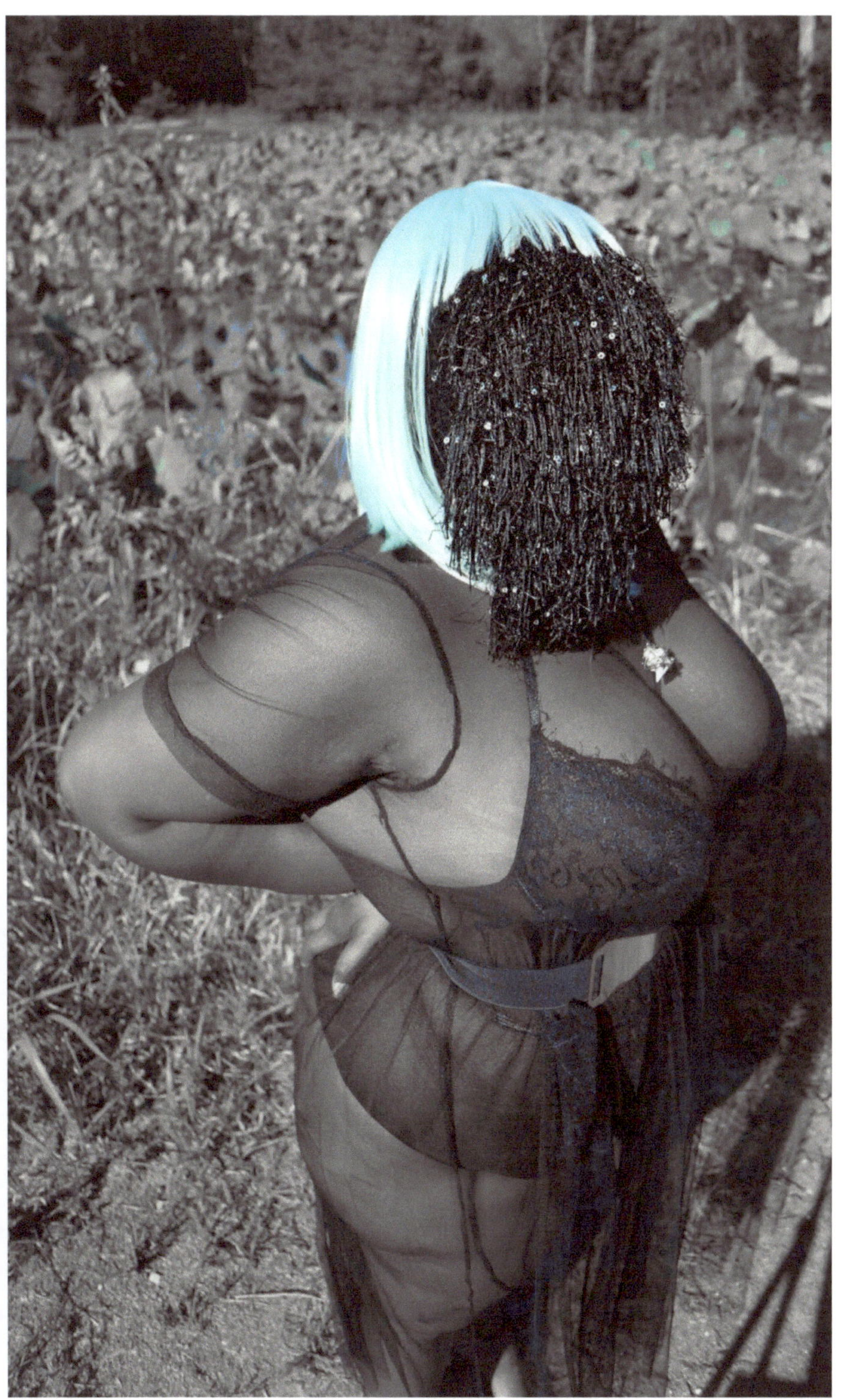

Dimensional haunting

Half the time I'm traveling dimensions. Dreaming lucidly, distorting memories, and merging alternate realities. Hard separating the 3rd dimension from the 5th dimension. Having a full life and family on one side and in constant battle with the same person on this side. Exasperating! How do I find balance? I hold my feelings in contempt, pretending they don't exist, but they resurface with a vengeance. I struggle every night. Resisting the visions produces aggressive infiltration of my subconscious. Full conversations with the deceased, telling me things you need from me, while I'm asking them, "Why I gotta be me to him?" A connection full of hauntings, one with the potential of knocking many people to their knees. Channeling strangers with no existence in the 3d. Does mourning for heartbreak of a relationship that never existed make me crazy? Weak? Imagine dreaming of the same person for two years every night. Misconstruing our interactions, folding under the intensity the time inopportune. Except for sex, must've been our love language in our past lives, and our daughter being the one thing we made right. Premonitions of holding her as you come through the door, dreams of talking with your parents while you're out on tour. Waking up in tears, the pain of vivid visions. Variations of our past life glitching. Am I the only person dreaming, or does your spirit reminisce too? Past life, and the regression continuously affects me. Is it Spirit maintaining the connection or is Spirit torturing me?

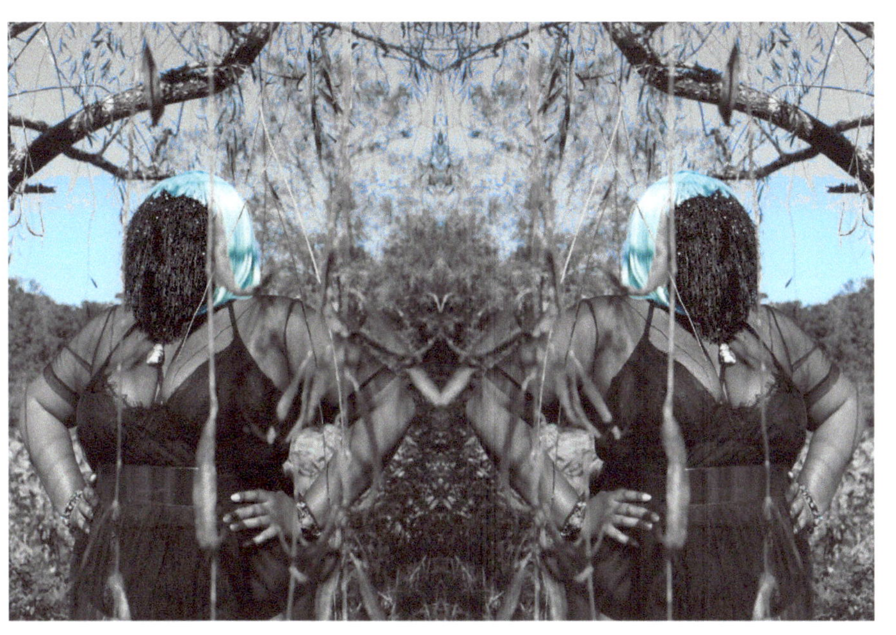

Red Nose Brigade

There looms a vile misconception within me. I promise my foolish ass behavior deserves an Emmy or whatever award they're giving clowns these days. Imminent disinterest, yet I still couldn't manage turning away. I never imagined identifying as a reformed red noser. Habitually forgiving my heart's betrayal until I unlearned how to give so much of me.

11 11

Do you remember we sat at the base of the cosmos as God begin coloring the sky? Egbe, our souls recognized each other. We consulted on the characteristics of beauty as the galaxies formed. In that moment, time meant nothing to us. As the moon enters phases every month, we return to our journey every time our souls meet. First lifetime separated by deceit. We lived in a garden and you deserted me. Compelling me to see all the flaws within us, causing the fall of humanity. Tore into every part of me, inciting bleeding freely, while you turned your heart away from me. Your misstep bore pain and remnants of our karma remain through every lifetime. Our second time incarnate you couldn't be with me. We lived on different sides of the railroad tracks. My family didn't have the money or status your parents looked up to. Third life you decided you weren't coming back with me, interesting how I always felt like a part of me was missing. The fourth time, you became me, and I personified you. We chose this journey to master the human experience of being in love with ourselves. You always took care of me. Fragments of our life puncture through to this plane. Your eyes still look the same, through them I can tell when you're in pain. I've always reached you that way, seeing through you but never saying much. Knowing that situations unraveled in their own time. Healing traumas accosting you. Fifth and sixth we separated. Learned without the other. We continued karma for ourselves, always finding a way to be near each other regardless of who we hurt, time, and distance. The seventh lifetime we were Spanish speaking moors. I ran a booth, and you ran your mouth per usual, but you intrigued me. We spent our teen years together but always remained friends. Eighth time we met in the 20s. It was my favorite era and lifetime with you. We sat next to each other at a wedding dinner, inseparable from that moment. I call it "love at soul recognition." You held me. We talked for hours. I fell asleep in your room seven nights in a row before you asked me to stay forever. We both were artists then too, you were more a renaissance man, and I, coincidentally wrote books. Ninth time we lived in the 50s and you weren't with me. You married someone else and had a baby girl. I balled every night for a year after I found out. Tenth time I told you I couldn't see you with anyone else. In exchange, we decided a fast track of having a daughter young ensuring we always maintain our connection. What exactly does this lifetime hold? I'm not sure but anytime life seems hard, I remember coloring the sky with you.

Fluency

I became fluent in your lies. Eloquently cherishing every good and well thing about you. Allowing a space of truth and virtues, not even your deepest love conceded. I finally understand process over feelings. The idea of loving professed through indifference. A dialect never spoken but you wanted the submission. I became fluent in your lies.

Silver tongue undressed the 4 chambers of my heart. Words decorated so elegantly with betrayals and false starts. Binding me with illusions, somehow my fluency predestined the breaking of me. Mistaking my projections for how easy our life could be.

I became so fluent in your lies; I obstructed my own eyes.

Conditional love

Unconditional love is a myth. My love has conditions that I'm treated the way I desire, nothing less. Or I walk away from people unapologetically. I believe people buy into unconditional love as a way of methodically misusing people. I left maltreatment at the beginning of 2020. Even God demands love a certain way. God doesn't force our love, but we risk lacking their mercy by not giving it. It's the same with me. There's no requirement people love or treat me the way I desire, but those actions risk releasing me from their life. I get it. As Jilly from Philly says, everything ain't for everybody. I'm the everything she talked about. Sometimes people just don't fuck with me and its ok.

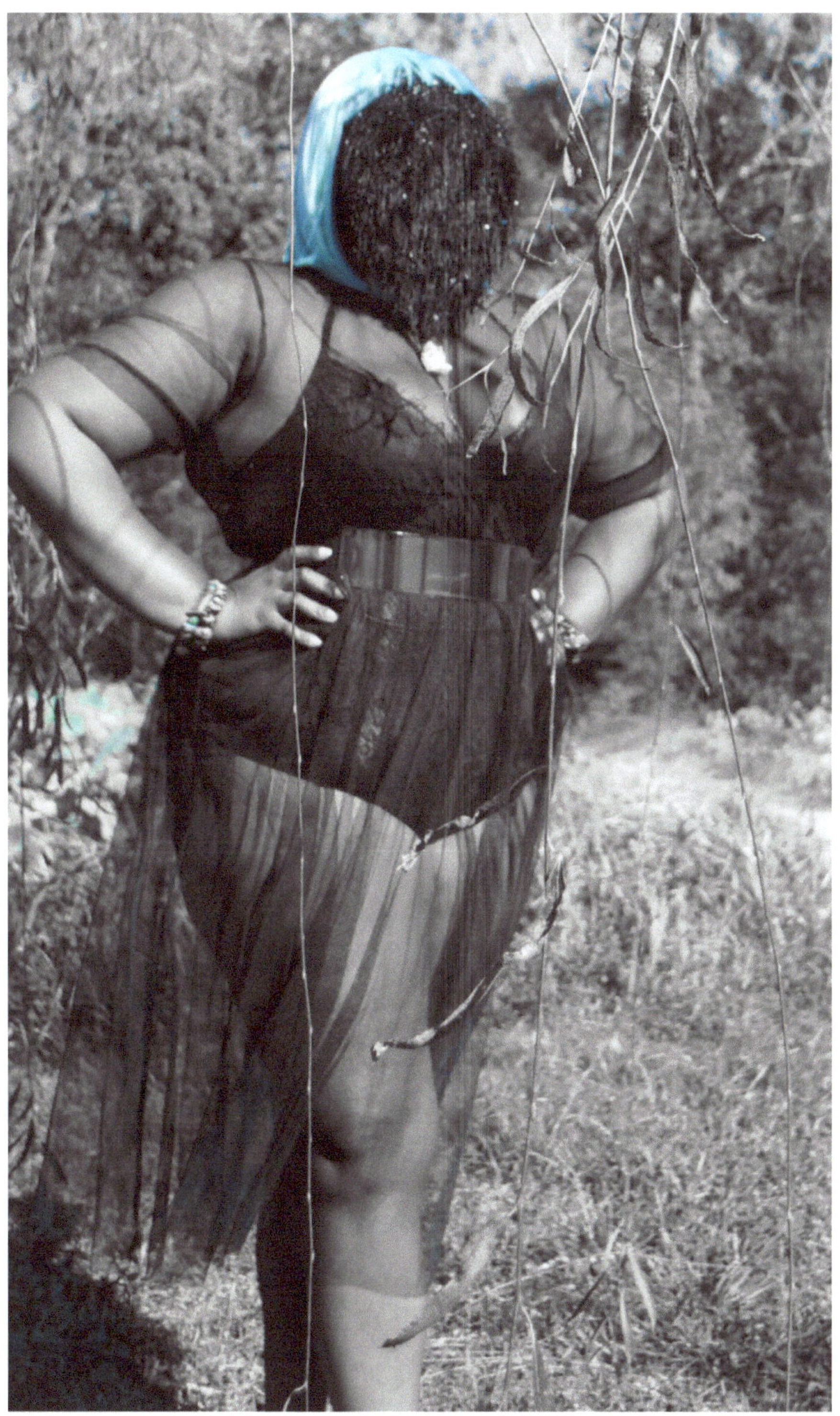

7 of cups

If your heart opens, you better have a sword for defense. People experience my spirit and become dependent on my energy. It's the empress residing in me. What happens when I let the anger out? What happens when you've hidden your shadow for so long, and she refuses returning to unseen? An encounter teetering at the seat of rage.

So, you'll get the cute, bubbly, unicorn. I'll deal with Ms. Sophie on the flip side. On a mission of protecting and healing my inner child since the age of five, dealing with unheard pain and wrestling with my self-esteem. A composition of hidden fantasies, gore, and anger but I only want the perception sweetness. Delightfully making my targets less suspecting. Not that a person risk danger around me. I truly reside in love. However, there's an atonement for disrespect, cuz my spirits don't play about me. Situations insinuate I'm the only person affected by the neglect and lack of love in this world. Standing in front of 7 cups and all of them overflow with pretenses of characteristics in you, my spirit beseeched me to receive in me. I saw love, talent, beauty, godliness, intelligence, work ethic, and perseverance. The cups spilled, clarifying you only craved me when I worked to your will. Spirit constantly tells me I come first. However, I'm riding on falsehoods that I'll never be seen. It's a gut punch meeting the reality of never being loved wholeheartedly. Spirit says I give too much, the sediments of trauma from never receiving enough love, attention, or time. So that's how I show my love, I over water. Irrigating my gifts, heart, and time through other people so much so that I ask, who will cry for me?

Options

From my experience and details of people around me some of my friends and I decided we need options. Unlearning putting all our eggs in one basket. We need a starter (our bottom bitch), a mechanic, a socialite, a carpenter, somebody with monies, a good dick slinger, an intellectual, a friend, and someone that likes to go on dates and talk shit. You feel me? 2020 feeling like these men for the streets!

Y'all don't pay me any mind. I'm just playing

Eh.

Maybe.

Dial Tone

Juju told me start divining on these men. I should've fucking listened, one was married, one had a live-in "friend", and one was just dick-fishing. It's crazy how my pussy told me let it be, but ol' boy talked heavy on his meat. I should've known then the only thing long on him was the deceit. I mean the absolute fucking nerve!

I asked before we went out, do you have a girlfriend, a bae, someone who thinks they're your bae, someone who would be mad right now if they knew you were talking to me? Are you gay? Each one of these mugs looked me in my eyes and said no. The live in confessed about his friend as if he told me what the deal was. The married one had two whole kids and one on the way. Y'all wanna know how I found out? In meditation, visions of him standing in a house, 2 kids wrapped around his leg and one in his arm with a bottle in their mouth. The crazy part was, he steadily plotted on making my day.

Sirrrrr clear my motherfucking line, I will not be a part of the national lampoon's family disarray. Shits wild out here. I'm spreading my wings, but the lack of honesty, honestly spoils it for me. I'd rather beat my meat, rub my own ass and go to sleep.

Seeds

I was once told that words don't hurt. Sharp tongues often yield pierced hearts. Words of love vibrate into awakenings. We elevate our life by speaking to our plants and praying over our food. Creating phases, worlds, outcomes, and reflections of the cosmos all within our thoughts and tongue. Speak intentionally.

Wounded Healer

I exhausted years pouring love into empty containers. I love freely and seek love returned the same way. Instead, there's a precedence of ones wanting blessings but void of sowing. Entertaining people who planted seeds to keep me, knowing that I could never leave my baby maturing in a world without a father. There was never any love for me. Satisfying an already inflated ego. "I respect you. I see you", when obviously you don't. Bragging to your homies about all the things you won't do. All because I wasn't the ideal archetype for you. How's that working? Experiencing the same type of woman in a different body when they all take you as a joke. How many hearts will you rupture? Ego provoked, so now you're rushing my way. Sade? Oh, that's bae? What, you thought I didn't know? As each blessing sprouts, you'll ponder on what you could've had as your pride burns slowly to the ground. Wishing possession, but never putting forth the effort of keeping me around. I could have helped you heal, foreseeing you as your higher self. You sought destruction of my confidence and intuition. Believing in past lives only when beneficial. Tainting and modifying me into you. A wounded healer, scared of love, afraid of intimacy, and walls as high as Mt Kilimanjaro. I forgive your imprints of sorrow and wasted time. Identifying my place in our issues. I'm embracing my pain, channeling the Magician, alchemizing these lessons.

I am that I am

I am, that I am

An expression not meant for everyone

An intention of understanding by those open to my vibration

Favor, entrusting love from a full cup

A celestial being commanding divine nastiness

Enchanting spiritually, energetically, and atomically

Spottieottiedopalicious

I hope I inspire living more fully. See how the sun and moon acknowledge you, skin embodying a looking glass of the deepest ethers. No mistaking you descended to Earth at its darkest moment, but light becomes you. "I can't wait to pour into you", those words seductively caress my ear drums, sending palpitations to a heart that took off its cool as you said, "let me be your lover." There's no desire of ownership, only a path of healing, love, magic and waves of ecstasy. Energy grand, compelling every word and thought felt, but regal enough to never have to say them. Grateful for shared moments, filled with abundance of intimacy and it was all before your lips ever devoured mine. I'm not easily moved but its humbling witnessing a manifestation epitomize God energy, while concentrating on bellows of melodic confessions of reverence. Past lovers could never quite attune to the melody. It's clear that every lesson before was my offering to the Divine that I could accept you easily as God's favor and protection. Teach me intimacy and I'll envelop you in romance. Every time you sing it's as if you conjure Obatala, Shango, and Orunmila, exonerating the roads to my heart, taking concern of my head, and linking your voice and my ears through intonations of heaven. Protect me physically, spiritually and emotionally and I'll bury it down for you in the spiritual realm. Procuring manna, we manifest sexually. Profoundly more vivid than our egos imagined. Presenting as a gift for this last year of soul lessons, I thank you for being you. DOPALICIOUS. Just in flo, ever so smoothly like a hot comb on virgin hair. I'm heavily intense but grateful that ain't all you see in me. Our gratuitous affinity ripples sound waves back 3000 years, signaling ancestral veneration as our moans reverberate, transmuting their deepest fears into loving energy.

OPEN.

YOUR.

EYES.

You tell me that lustfully as I witness your eyes roll into the abyss of your most pleasurable thoughts while filling me with extensions of Spotieottiedopaliciousness. Incense burning, souls kissing, and rhythms of our yin and yang echo like oiled handprints on beige walls. Intertwined in each other's limbs as our higher selves recall life in heaven before the fall.

Expectations

Imagine that, my expectations left me expecting.

Untilled Garden

Sometimes I listen our voice notes laced with the journey from friend to lover. Although there is no one I speak with all the time, I miss you, every day. Overshadowed by past lovers who could not accept my fullness. Remedying a life outside of other people's judgements. Take count of everything starving your dreams. Stop living in the overgrown mediocrity of other's secret garden. Snap the vines of distortions infiltrating your mental walls. How the hell are you listening to someone who ostentatiously tills their garden? A walking, living, energetic disappointment. When you're empathic, minor things can seem like an overreaction to the destitute. This is no sneak diss. Disproportionately feeding their gardens while they poison your intuition. Sometimes the very thing nourishing us can leave our spirits emaciated. How are you dealing with the ramifications? At some point you digested their supposition as truth. Battling internally because you've grown in love with me, recognizing real oxidizes untruths. May every time you recall your lips touching mine summon a flow of sweetness, incite inspiration and heal the wounds of never being allowed to waver in the depths of your own love.

Interesting

You squander your manifestations? Interesting.

The Room of Requirement

Why do we petition what we're not ready for? Men full of nuances, constantly seeking power over the divine feminine, simply uninspired in their existence. Words convoluting like staircases of everchanging stances. Standing up to you always leaves me questioning me. "Who are you?" I'm whoever the fuck I'm envisioning. The expansion of my spirituality romanticized rising in love with you. Instead, our connection mimicked the most desolate love song, a descending crescendo entitled defense against the dark arts. All the love that exists inside of me, consuming, too much to horde. I voluntarily give it away. Loyal, but depleted in you betraying me. Echoes of my future self-seeping through, allowing "friends" to steal your magic, siphoning your value. I'll never condone your exploitation. Stop fucking with people who can't comprehend your spirit. Using you as a step stool cuz they recognize your power way before you had a chance to concede to the higher you. Deserving a life of divine existence. I guess I can't be upset when I'm living in my highest guidance of healing. Resembling the Mirror of Erised, reflecting one's deepest desires.

PTDD part 2

Post Traumatic Dick Disorder Part Two

Honestly, I deserve better. Will I ever reach indemnification for the love given, or will I forever be stuck in a paradox of men who say they love women but do everything to ruin their spirits?

Fear

What's my greatest fear? Previously it was never experiencing the fullness of love. Now it's not completing my soul work. Our human experience distracts us. It's a labor of love reprogramming oneself from pain. I no longer validate myself through the eyes of other people. Do I like me? Do I fuck with me? And damn if I love you, do you love yourself? Cuz that's a whole 'nother level that I'm not willing to carry. We'll meet in the middle of completing our soul work. No more emotional Trojan horses, I will not allow myself to be an emotional rehabilitation center.

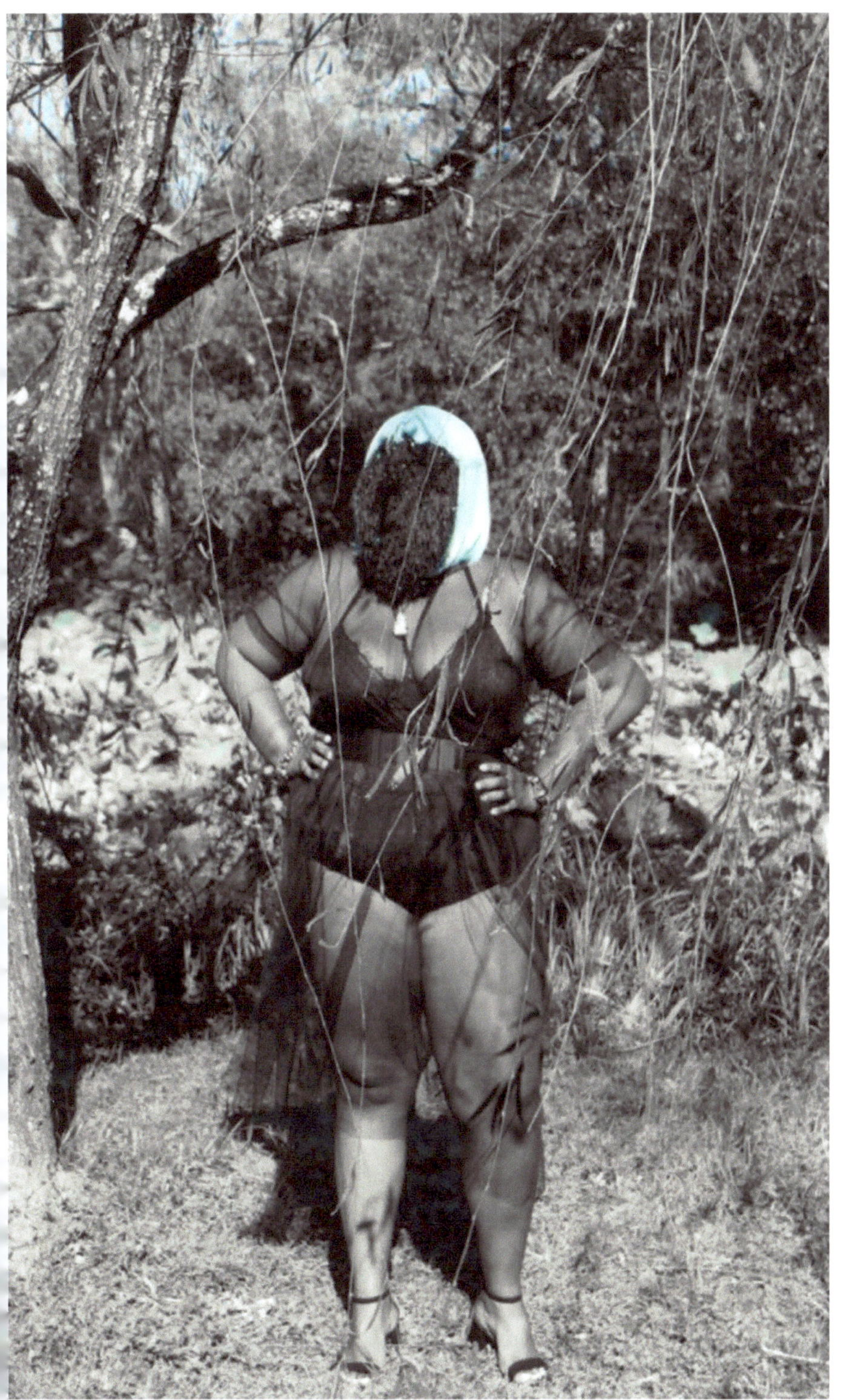

Heal her Blues

Energy

Kindness

Fury

Overwhelmed

Hurting

Seductive

Horny

Emotional

Magnetic

Sleepy

Slept On

Ascending

Alien

Un FUCK With Able

My head ain't the only thing about me bringing conscious tips, go through whole awakenings by experiencing dimensions of my full lips. I've existed at least three lifetimes without you, which lets me know I was whole before ever giving the Universe permission to split my soul and make you.

UNFUCKWITHABLE

Now am I your trophy or are you mine? Never wanting to taxidermy our connection for conversation or seem unkind to a soul that mirrored mine because that would be just like you, abandoning me! Love should change us for the better. I pray that I never let the actions of others debilitate my sweetness. I'm realizing loving hard is okay, the problem comes when I try controlling the outcome of what loving hard means. I should love you either way because I recognize so much of myself. Running laps in my own head as to why I can never come at you again. I can never get upset at a sleeping God. Are you sleep because you didn't pick me? No, you're sleep because you're blind to the illusion that other women could ever be me and conjure up what I have for you. They're just playing magical with their house brooms. Just like those three lifetimes I must continue existing without you, heal this world like a piece of my soul never existed, cuz this time I'm living without you in an honorable existence. Build my nice home, sunflower gardens, enjoy these herbs and raise these chickens.

UNFUCKWITHABLE

I'm sweet

I'm kind

I'm talented

I'm hilarious

I'm a wealth magnet

I'm sexy

I'm intelligent

I'm feminine

I'm nasty,

Fuck you sweetly, edge you off then fix you something to eat. Not just for your belly but soul comfort, as if you're conversing with your nanny. Ever see Goddess enjoy creation in its purest form? Queening you erupts my honey jar into the manna of heaven as your face absorbs every drop, your third eye still processing all that you could be. My love will change you and you'll wonder why you'll search for me in every woman, only perpetuating a lie of thinly veiled soul ties. You haven't been nice; you haven't been a friend, it's a wonder I don't call on my ancestors to break your ass in. But I got to stay balance because a true Goddess never reacts with malice. Only responding with a swift act of the sword, knowing it'll teach you more when I sever this etheric cord. UnFUCKWITHABLE

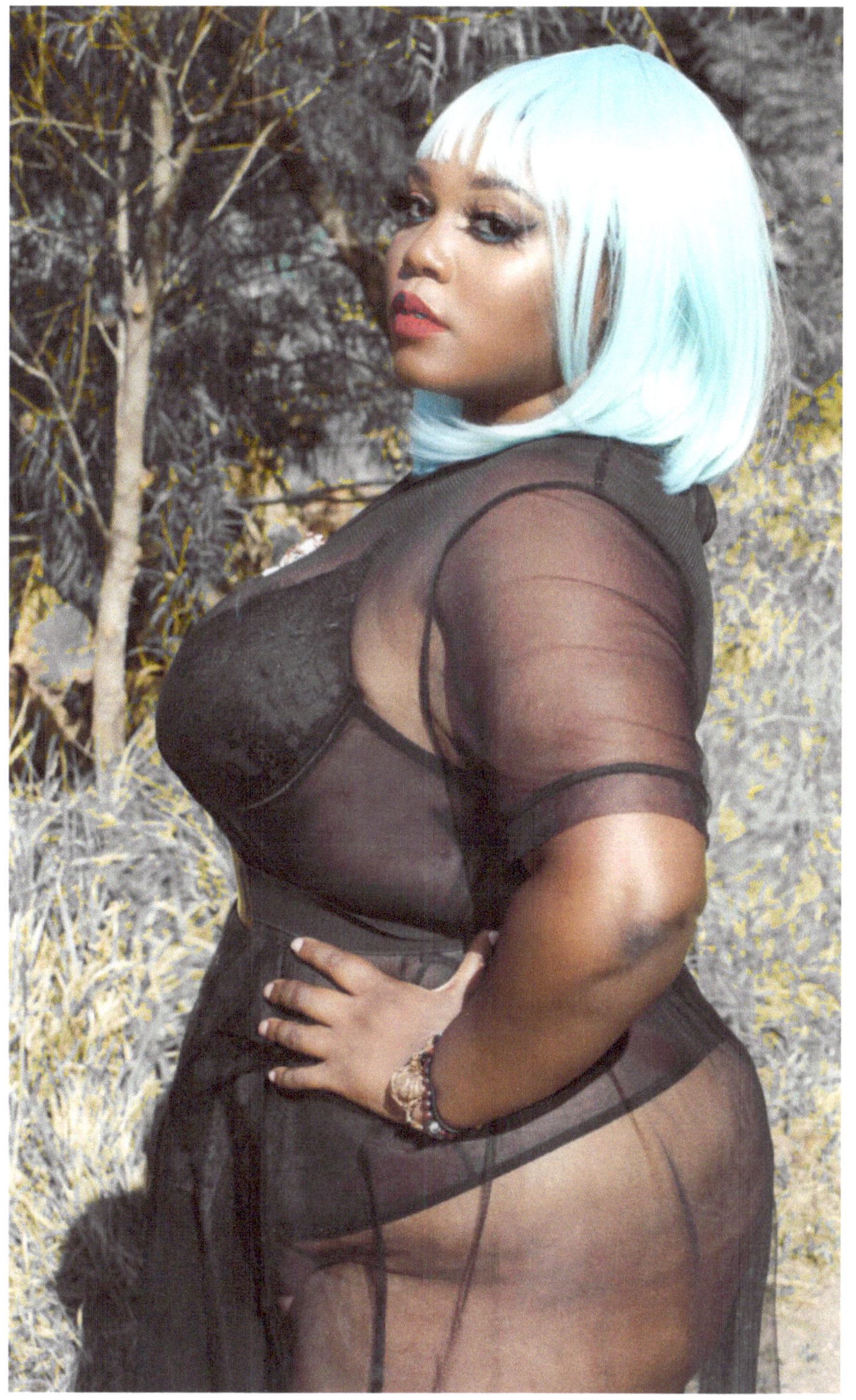

Otherworldly

I woke up one morning feeling otherworldly. I can't change that about myself. The gift of our lives resides in interconnectedness. Experiencing people deeply uncovers the innermost parts of ourselves. The journey recalibrates by finding some people can't love the way I love because they only know love from their perspective. I will love anyway, but I will love me unforgivingly.

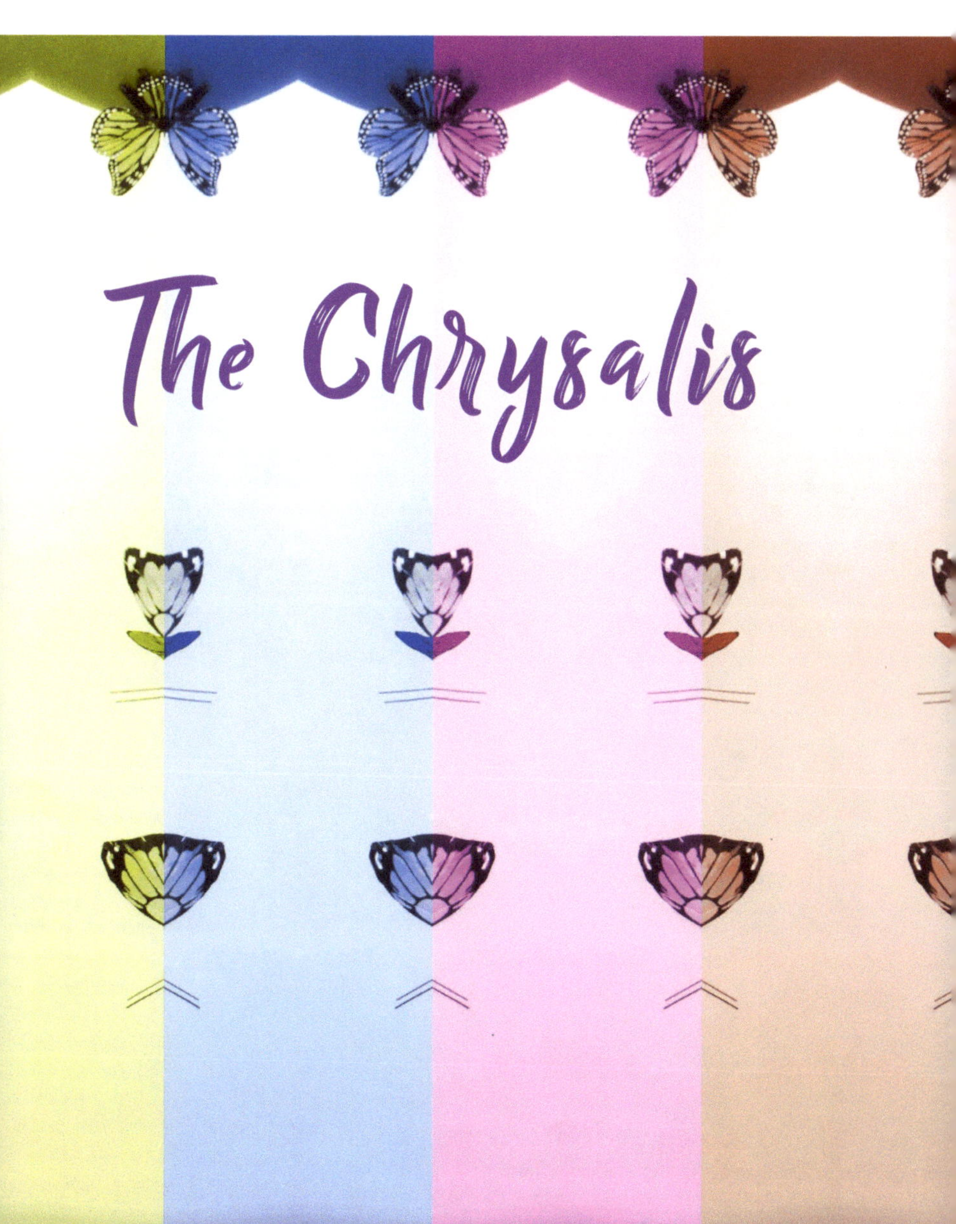
The Chrysalis

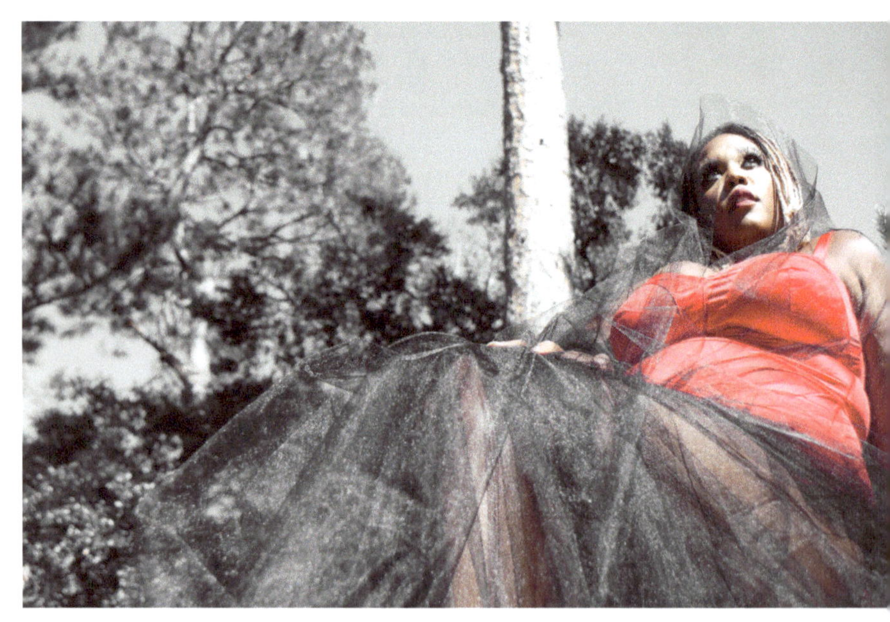

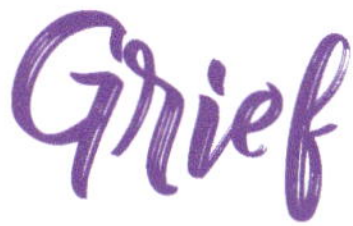

Grief rolls in waves. Monumental layers of grief triggered by a thought, sound, smell or touch. Death thought to be when a person no longer exists in this dimension. I learned that sometimes in death, a person lives but no longer operates the same way.

Hallow Moon

Do you know how death feels? Unhinged, meticulous and piercing. Self-absorbed, simulating falsehoods of isolation. I went to my funeral at least 4 times this year. Here lies my emotional body. At its lowest, pouring from an empty cup, enlightened that no is a two-letter sentence. Mulling over misunderstandings preluding my demise. Self-betrayal cuts deeper than any romantic discord. Lost in the wake of my physical body, shedding the miseries of my reflection. Now slaying self-deprecating behaviors, affirming unconditional body love. Radical intentionality, accepting that my belly means I eat good, in a world where nip/tucks standardize "self-care acts." Rejoicing in the whirlwind of my rolls, riding the roads of self-love. Each curve caravanning my nieces, as they find comfort in their nanny's arms. Death left me disassociating with those pandering for validation. Fallacy. I died at least four times this year, rising from the ashes anew and rebirthed as the woman overcoming multiple deaths and using my tears as a healing tincture for Spirit. Many truths but the most important, what I believe of myself. I died at least four times this year and regenerated as a butterfly.

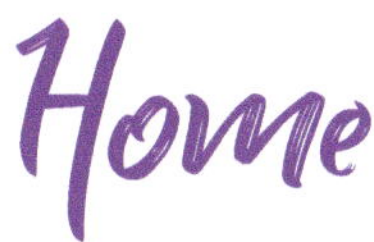

Home is wherever I am because, I carry my home with me.

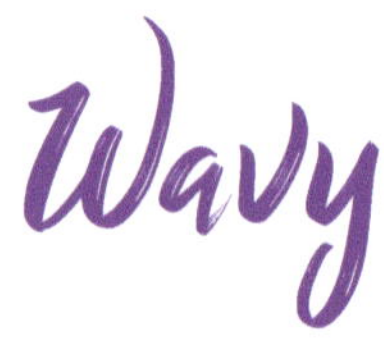

When I need tranquility it's the water I run to,
it's no coincidence that you are composed of
about 70% of it. Even when cold, your ice caps
still provide value. That's Lani pas, an exploit only
tripling in value once you see it for yourself. As
the water commands, so do you, never teaching
people how to handle you. They'll soon learn you're
a personification of Earth's spirit, airy calmness,
captivating enough to drown, a fiery reckoning,
holy enough to cleanse. Weeping as my soul
becomes lost in the chaos of the world, the ocean
emulates my church. Water, grounding and a
pseudo womb. Blessed as the butterfly seeking an
ancestor's kiss. Baptismal rebirth of resounding
intuition. Welcoming my power, becoming my own
oracle, my own historian, for generations before
and the ones birthed from me. As temperamental
as the waves abounding the shore, when I need
peace, it's the water I run to, it's no coincidence
that I go within to find you.

Its Not Over

Healing is not a single occurrence. Healing mimics a broken ankle. A broken ankle is casted, it hurts but you know the pain is necessary. Then when it rains it aches. Aches resemble reminders of our triggers. Identifying parts that still need mending. I call this process shadow work, leading us to pluck the root of our issues. Correlating our issues with our traumas assists us in creating better boundaries.

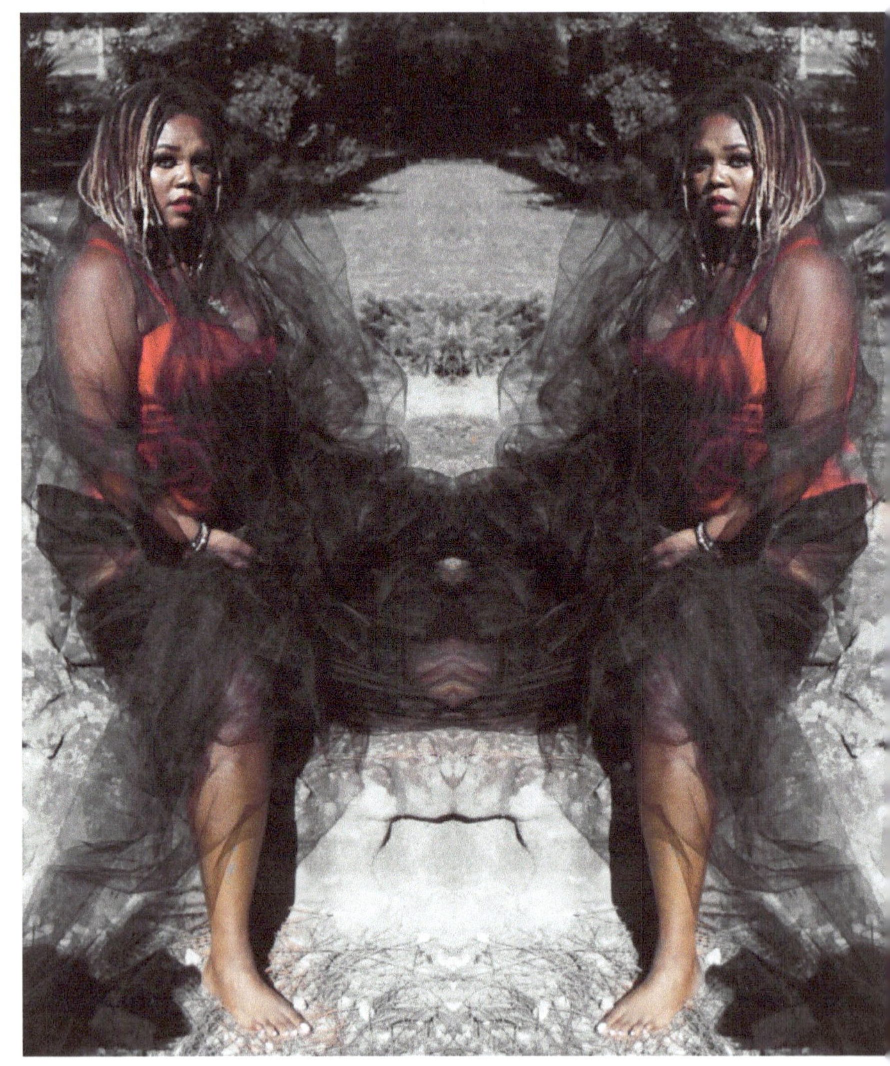

Vampires

I bought the lesson of welcoming my ruin. Assessing the lack of seriousness in your pursuit, and I respect your stance but I'm in a position where I can't play about me. Disparagement hitting abruptly, paying the price for gifting pieces of me. I'm reconstituting my devotion. People mutate into vampires around me, swear they don't like me, concisely harvesting my energy. Parasitically resembling carcasses of their enemy. A staple of purity, even my tribulations make room for me. The discord forms a gaping hole, opening my heart for room to breathe, stretch and grow. A journey of preservation, mastering self-love.

Problem Child

After thee drama clears, I'm left swimming in emotions. Overthinking and worrying how my actions affect others when that same consideration doesn't extend towards me. I accept I'm the common denominator of my problems.

Forgiveness

Losing trust in myself parallels war crimes against humanity. Kaleidoscope views, ingesting fragmented lenses of how people loved me. In healing people speak of the betrayal of others, but never the betrayal of self. How can I expect the bound to rejoice for the free?

I forgive you.

Excuse me, I'm having a heart to heart with me. I forgive myself for feeling played. I couldn't see the height of my magnetism. Mercifully releasing myself from a repository of empty promises and never reserving that patience for myself. I forgive me for casting my pearls upon swine, knowing I spiritually transform minds. I forgive me for diminishing my Goddess energy. Brooding over decisions that undermined my intuition, fragile boundaries, all in the spirit of helping people I love with their healing. Self-betrayal evokes retribution, magnifying my imperfections of not being a resident in my own heart chakra. Most of all, I forgive myself for exploiting my intercession.

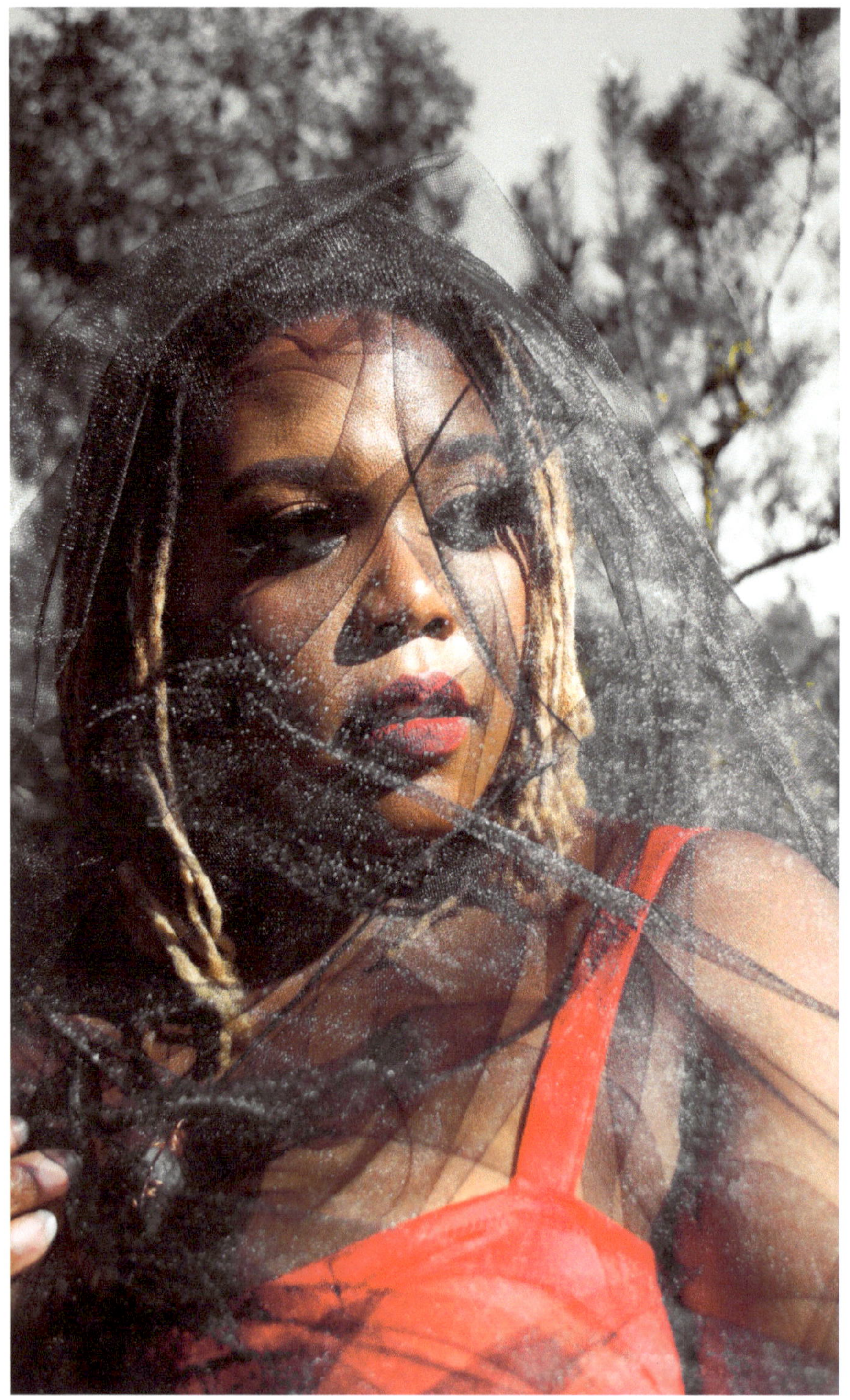

Choices

There comes a certain point in self-actualization where the healing starts to hurt again. Our journey sharpens us, but we always have a choice in standing in our power or giving it away.

Mirrored NRG

Mirror, you reflect my truths. Healing our relationship extracted my ugly parts too. Revealing I could be manipulative, unkind, and self-serving. Reveling in my dark feminine nrg, unveiling scars that stretch past our connection. Convinced, I too am an arsonist, burning down things that get close, so I took some time repairing my thoughts and emotions. As I apologized to me, this serves as penitence in my actions towards you. I regret hearing but not listening to your gentle truths, impeding on your free will, and manipulating the situation from my emotions at the time. I never acted with ill intent. Covering you spiritually, but I understand the malice of intervening without your consent. I innately protect people precious to me. New to my power, unfamiliar to the feeling of wanting a person as much as I want to breathe. Too much responsibility for any person to carry. I fed into the twin flame hype, a juxtaposition of our energy. Resembling my home, but you were hell bent on leaving me homeless. Igniting a flame of loving with my whole heart, but I never affirmed to the universe that I wanted you to love me. A compilation of emotional regurgitation, overly understanding, overly forgiving. A connection made for upgrading soul development. Lessons never make situations easy. My fascination with you kept me from aiding you in my High Priestess energy. A challenging reminder that I'm the cornerstone of having love more abundantly. I appreciate your forgiveness and really value the maturity, as neither one of us are really that easy to understand. Complex and headstrong, all the while repressing a million feelings. It's difficult severing an ethereal connection, especially when a person consoles the parts others view as unbearable. Gauging me better than I can measure myself. Unearthing the most ancient parts of a love I buried. Grateful for our soul's reintroduction. So, instead of dwelling on all that has broken, I'll focus on rebuilding and sharing love platonically.

Cardiology

I refuse to let this world make me bitter. I only aim to love like I never loved before and with childlike trust.

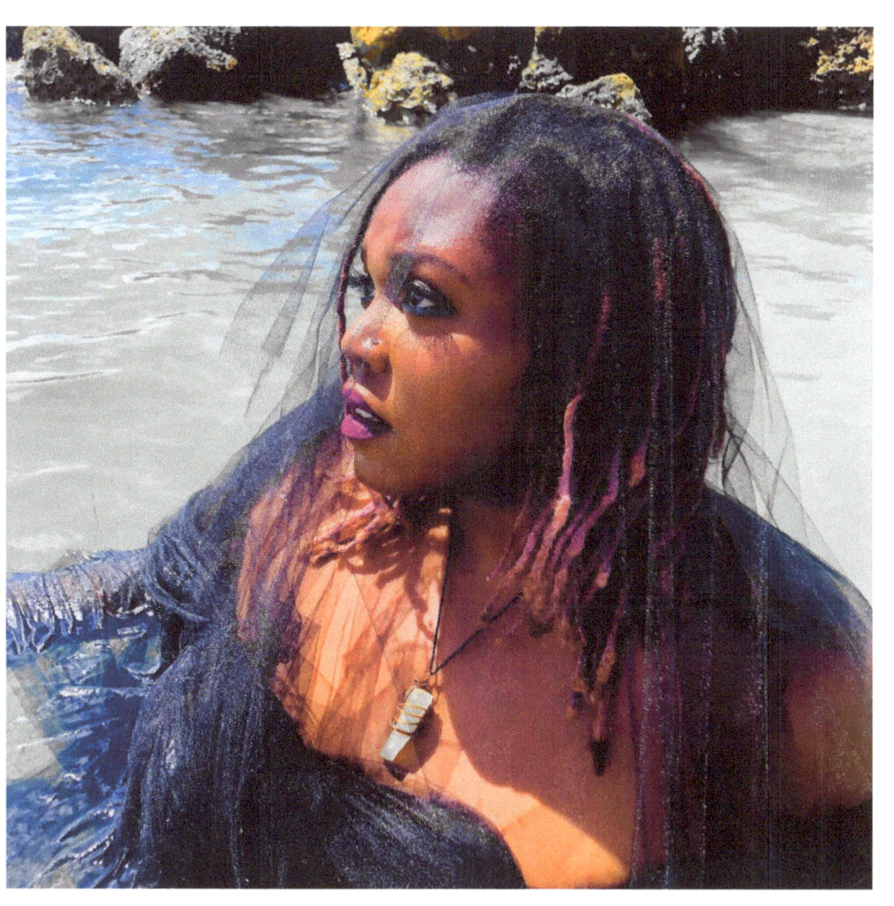

Be safe with me

Men yearn too. Clear that motherfucking throat chakra cuz holding back only hurts you. I told you a million times, if I take your feelings personally that's a trigger pining for attention. Yes, I understand that money makes the world go around but profit doesn't outweigh sacrificing our soul. I'm aware we can't survive off love alone. I uplift your efforts of living in your gifts. Working in our passions aligns us to the Universe. There's a misalignment existing between what I think of you and how the world treats you. I'm so proud of you. Proving your promises of every-time you see me you'll come back better. You exceeded abundantly, outside of me you already found the source of legacy. I wasn't forcing you into building with me, reinforcing the proclamations of us sharing energy. Remember you're always safe with me.

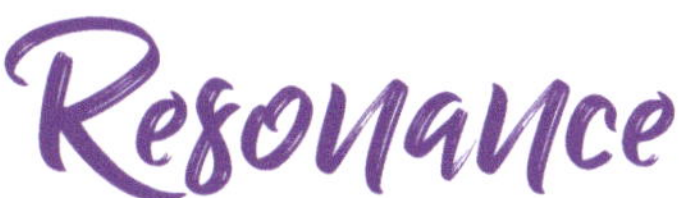

We must not shift based on other people's vibrations.

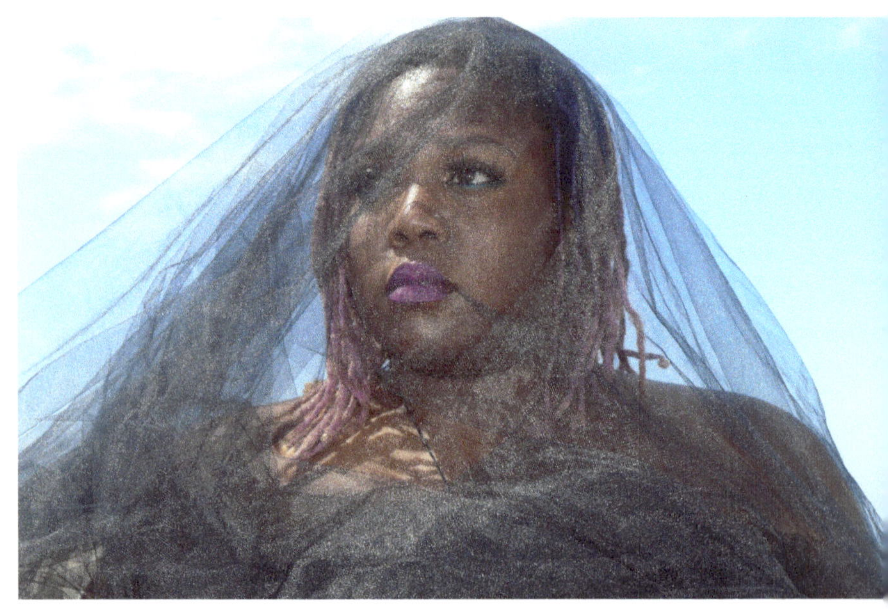

The Chrysalis Theory

Cocooning requires letting things fall away.
Alchemizing my strands of doubt, despair into
worth, forgiveness, and celibacy. My woes, a
steppingstone to the manifestation of a new
me. Wrapping my affirmations like silk, birthing
tranquil peace. A perceptive solitude. How can
our souls learn love constantly surrounded? So,
like a caterpillar I'll anchor myself, but instead of
fastening upon a tree, I'll anchor myself to me.
We often wish for beauty but never hip ourselves
to the destruction required in metamorphosis.
Sacrifice covers half the battle. Rejecting all
delusions my spirit consumed because this next
phase of life requires food palatable to the 5d.
I'm ascending, eradicating thoughts of who I was
previously. Taking inventory of what deserves to
stay. Healing and dissolving all my ugly parts away.

The Butterfly

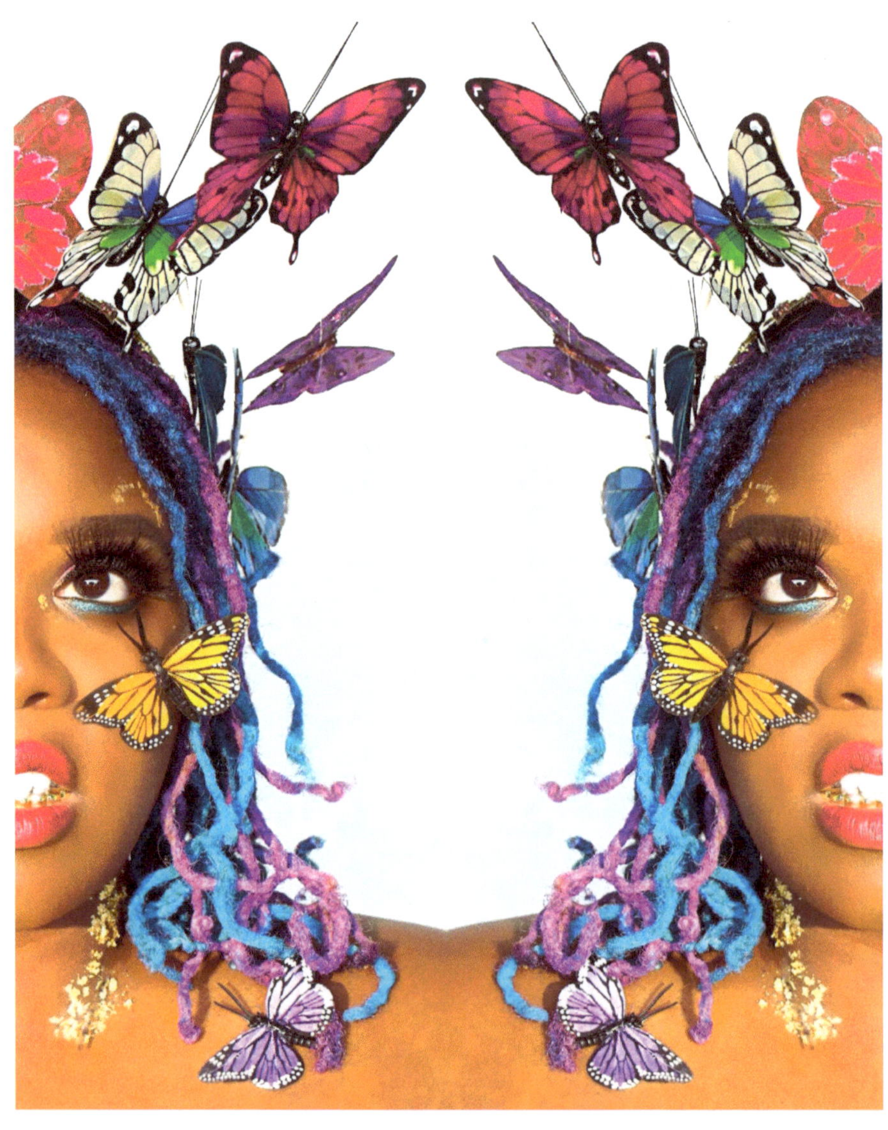

Attraction

When you look for the beauty in everything you can see the beauty in everything. I empathize with bitter people. Working through my hurts helped acknowledge men as a blessing, as a divine counterpart. A certain level of growth is required to resolve trauma and imagine people from a higher perspective. 2020 prompted a longing for more easiness in my life. We must remain vigilant in our request. Receiving ease in a connection triggered me. I found myself fumbling for words because the interaction didn't require defensiveness. Sharing love with a person, and we hold space for love, where things don't have to be difficult. I'm also learning ease with loving myself more.

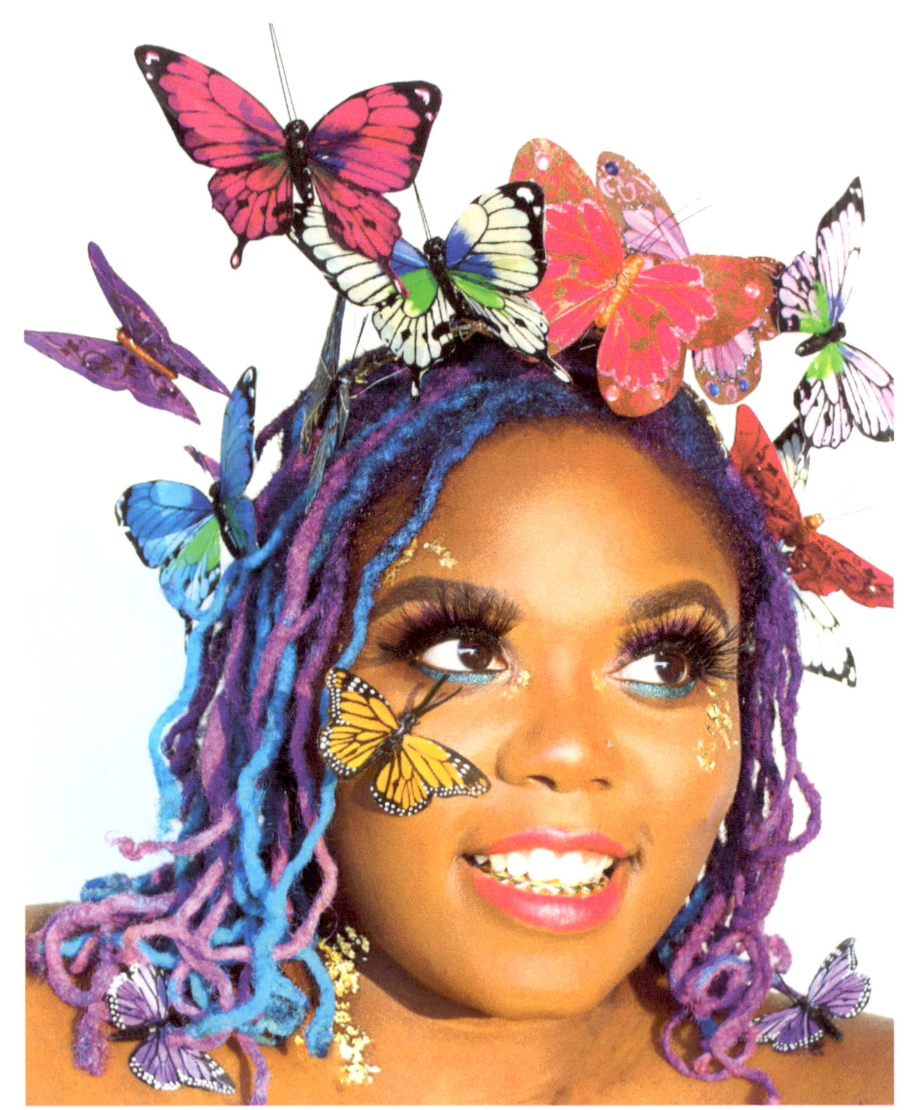

Gratitude

I arose with the sun and said my prayers,
Thanked the ancestors for divine protection,
meditated on my fears, released some shit I hadn't
acknowledged in years. My angels confirmed peace
by ringing joyful noise in my ears. Pandemic got
me overworked, in my feelings, planetary actions
pulling up years of hurt. In front of my altar, putting
in work. Readings, reiki, a lil graveyard dirt. Asé to
Annis.

Psalms 91 one to cover me, ancestors speaking
through me. Taking my ascension seriously,
venerating my family.

My granny turned 99, and one day I'll be just as
fine. Focused when I manifest, and I really do
deserve the best. Dreams overtaking me, gifts
passed through the women in my family, a lineage
of high priestess energy,

My ancestors reside within me. Here's my first
encounters with divinity:

Winnie,

Mary,

Lettice,

Antionette,

Karen,

Sister,

Donna,

Claudetta,

Marlo,

Y'all paved the way.

Empress in my family, abundance revealed through me, in alignment to mastery. Love all around me, living life effervescently.

Soul food

In case you were wondering, yes, I am soul food, whole moods, a fucking sweetheart, OG unicorn, high key genius, Fashion connoisseur, quirk enthusiast, kinky ass lover with steal your soul kisses, mythical southern lady, high vibing, crystal child, energy healing, hoodoo studyin', God lovin Goddess.

Hur Confers A Crwn

Savor my exotic essence. Reminiscent of Honey with a splash of habanero. Sweet enough to reel you in but sultry enough to warm you for winters entirety. Submissive enough to let you enter my heart space, dominant enough to make you plead. See I am the bee's knees, a walking manifestation of my own honey jar. Roots don't work on this strange fruit. Protected even when I'm rejected, see the knowledge soon come. High John in my satchel has been fed with a taste of smoke and rum, which means I always got that good juju. Raised up in a church blinded to its own sanctity. It only took losing me, being baptized in my own iniquities to see I was already born into divinity. The veil soon come, my eyes soon see, everything Source was divinely teaching me. I had to get out of my own way. Let mama Oya clear the path, and papa Shango overcome the mountain of every obstacle laid before me. To understand free, you must understand servitude, that's why you'll always catch me with the humanitarian attitude. When I see my sister it's just a projection of myself, and when I see my brother, I see my strength and my weakness. That's why I must remain free. Cast light to heal masculinity, deal with my own masculine energy. For everything in this world requires synergy.

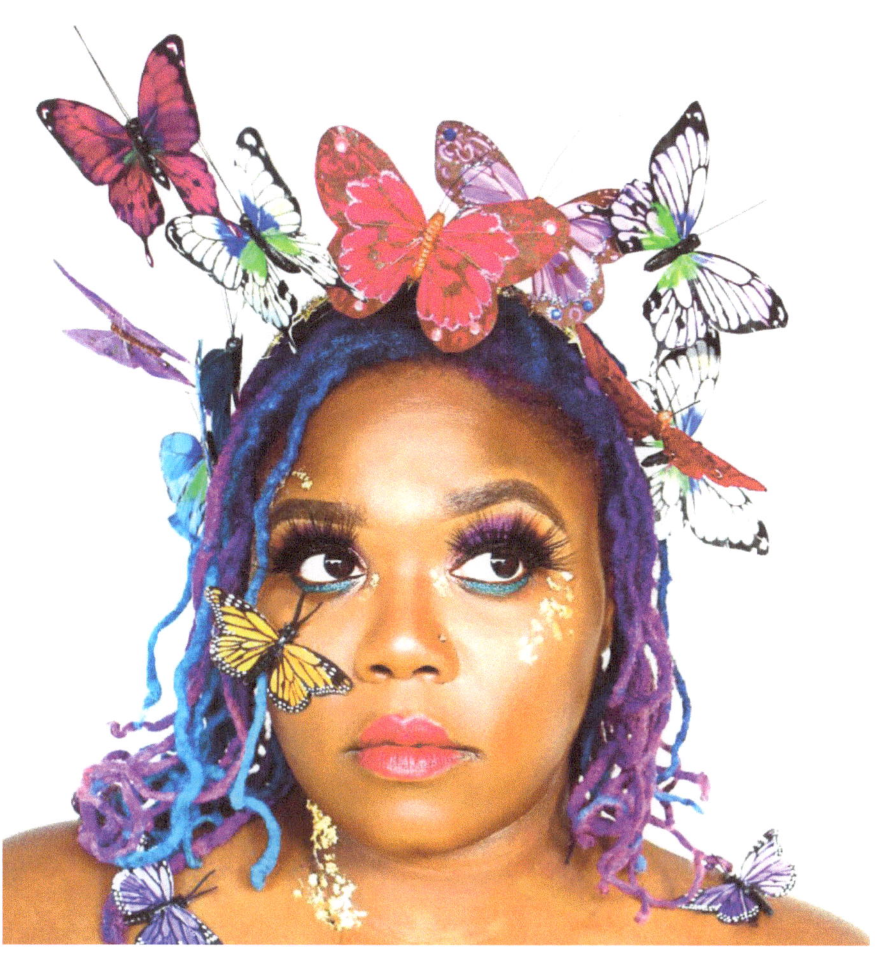

Free

I aspire freedom in all areas of my life. Nothing compares to those moments of liberation. Peace, freedom, and living in flow are the keys of an unapologetic life. Someone once told me don't become too free that I lose how to love. I realize I could never do that. Love exudes the most freedom. Think about it, I can love anyone in this world and they never have to love me back or even know I love them? How divine is it loving without fearing reciprocity? No one can control that kind of love.

Goddess Pussy Energy

I don't want a dick pic. I want to hear you moan from the depths of your belly summoning all that sacral energy. Healing, emanating soul symmetry. It's the morning nut videos for me. Baby show me you rise thinking about me, visually feasting on all that dick Imma get today. Put me on your calendar bae, 4 'til we finished. Douse me in auditory waves of pleasure while I accompany the rhythm of your arousal cycle. Lay back, learn to receive, while I blow you shotguns as I get high off your pre cum. Attune to my yoni, channeling Epithymia and Peitho, goddesses ensuring you'll always crave more. Are you fulfilled? Grab the rope babe, don't let our trip to Dom Depot be in vain. I trust you. Come close but ask for permission. Get face to lips with my pearl. Linguistically detail your love notes. You ask, "Vous, vous plaisez?" As I reply, "J'aime ta bouche." Meditate on her, she requires transcendental mindfulness. Digitally assault me, five is the magic number. Serve my sweetness off your fingertips. Splash marks the spot, drink me like the fountain of youth. Enter me with that past life intimacy, merging with my life force. Align with me. Ritually, I innerstand you prefer it filthy. Wrap your hands around my throat like kundalini rising. Bite me. Spank me and watch it bounce back. Own me. Spit in my mouth, let me drink it

as a sacrament. Tell me some overly nasty shit
as I submit. Each stroke releases my heart, the
reflexology of fucking. I beg you to come, as I feel
light burst around me. Let me catch each thrust for
you, I mean that nut for you. Prayers exist in many
forms, so we say grace over each other's bodies.
Glaze me like twelve donuts from your favorite
place. Confess you worship me. We evoked the
spirit of sex and I'm your sacred space.

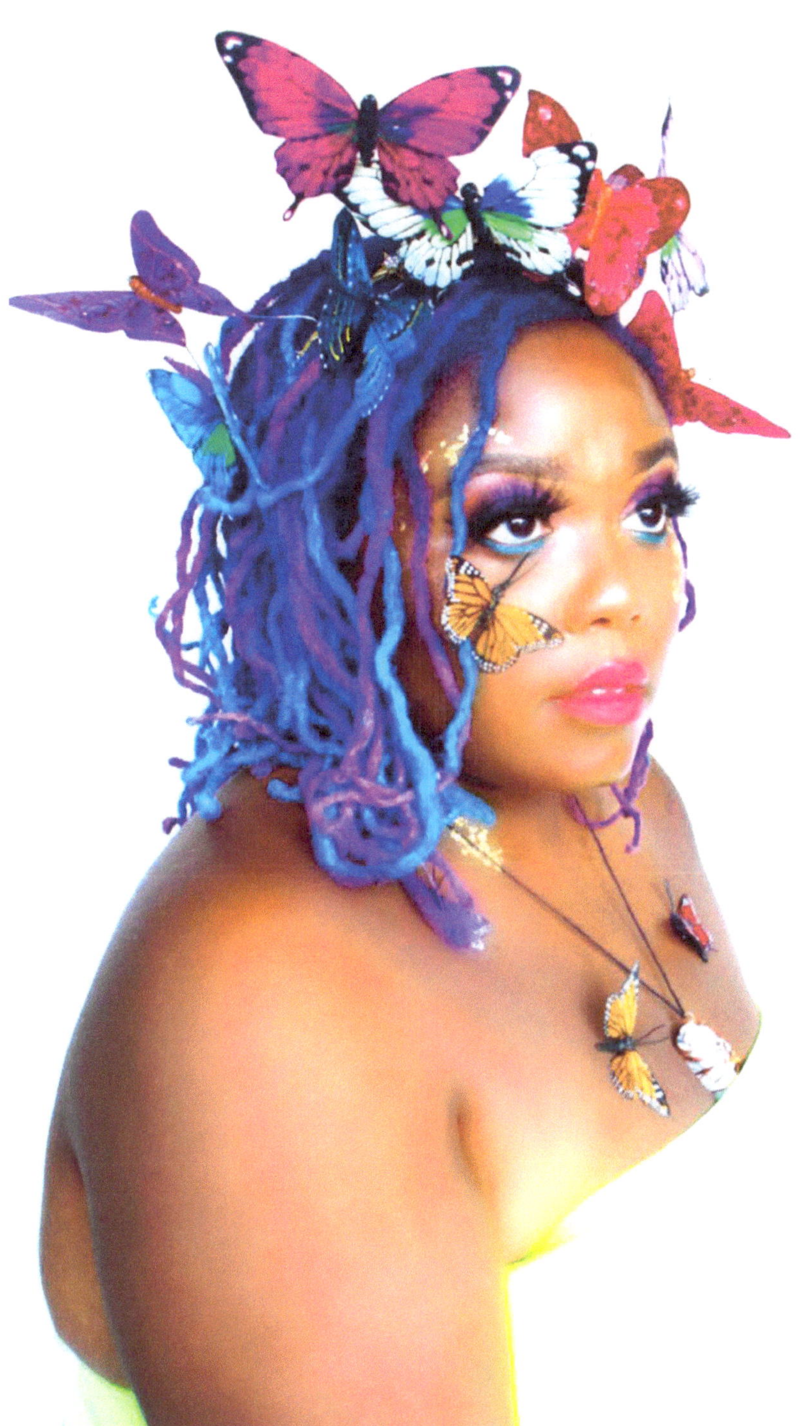

Radical Pleasure

Pleasure exudes one of the simplest ways of self-worship. I enjoy the intimacies of being a lover and learning my lover. I believe if people live outside of the thoughts of other people there would be way less anxiety and heartache surrounding pleasure and sex.

Oracle

Head so good he knows when I miss him, I'm gone step to the mic, splendidly orating vibratos of pleasure. Laying offerings of my mouth, I kiss his hip, inscribing Psalms of Elegua, each flick of my frenulum opens the door to other worlds, welcoming his dick with manifestations. Insatiable desires of tasting him. Two hands, one on his shaft, one playing keys on his perineum. As our breaths sync, each slurp, spit, stroke and ahhh fuck become our soundtrack. Every pulsation fills me with a streak of power, his veins lay the roadmap to his treasure, never choking, bringing forward emollients of lust. Let's write out our desires, and place them under our crown, so we conjure more than just our babies. When his dick jumps, it convinces me that I'm at the right place, at the right time, standing between heaven and devouring his soul. Intergalactic loving. Let's fuck on Jupiter's 79 moons and declare it gospel for the universe. We lock eyes and I know he's slowly melting into the abyss of 14 types of orgasms a man can have, and he's halfway to six. I hum a tune while his moans play in minor key. To an untrained ear, that may sound melancholy but to me it's laced with emotional intensity. His toes crack, tsunamis of explicit epithets placate his mouth, releasing pressure, almost completing my quest down south. His body convulses, balls disappear, meat grows harder as I render erotic cadences on his tip. Taking his nut back, my shot of tequila, canvassing his phalas for any drop I've missed, remnants of lust drip down my lips, as I pull him in to give a kiss.

Manifestations

It's time to love again. Universe, this time I want it to be fully reciprocated. A love so bright that it heals the love wounds for others. Protective and ensuring everyone knows he doesn't play about me. Universe, a love so big, fun, and innocent that we act like kids together. A love so passionate it makes the most sensual person blush. A long-standing love that our kids aspire to have. A love full of friendship, a safe space for our darkest secrets. A love full of freedom and wildness. A love who owns his power, so he doesn't feel intimidated by me standing in my own. A poetic love, caring, romantic, partnership, traveling, adventurous, a supportive, a family-oriented, communicating, you mad sit your ass down so we can fix it, faithful, prosperous, sexy, open, fine ass, dressing ass, spiritual love. A divine love.

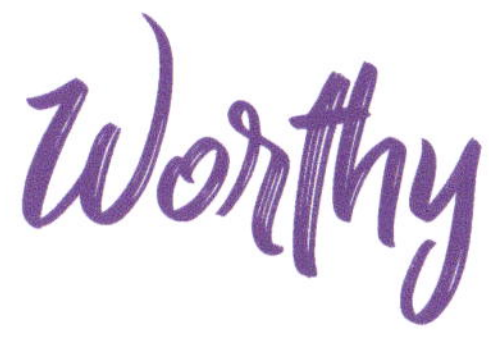

A proclamation of worthiness.

No longer toiling over ideas of what makes me worthy.

I honor myself.

Through the brightness of my eyes

The dip in my Cupid's bow

The joy in my laughter

The love in my heart

The gratitude in my rising

The wildness in my spirit

The gentleness in my hugs

I know that the worthiness radiates from within me.

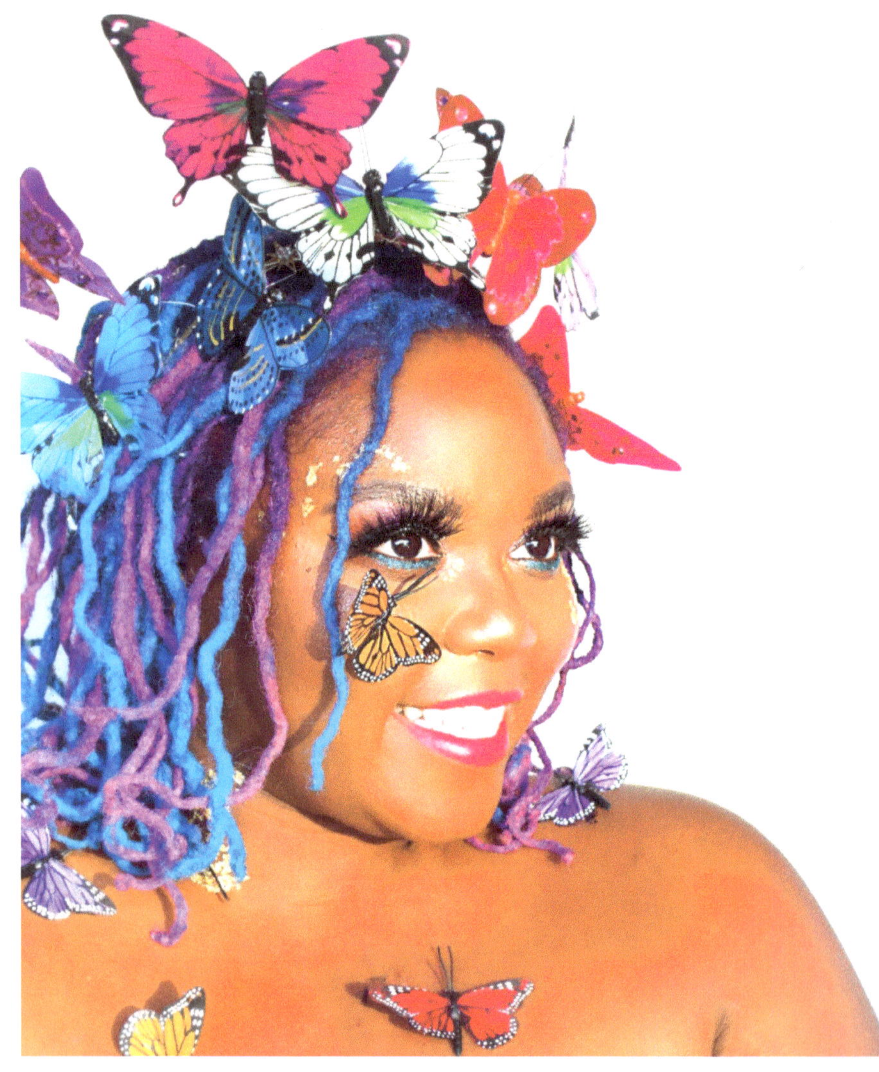

Divine Connection

In tarot, The Lovers represent divine connection between feminine and masculine energies. I'm both fortunate and unfortunate to have met my twin flame. I also met divine connections, or soulmates. The encounters inspired me.

The Lovers

Divine Feminine to Divine Masculine

Have you ever met someone who upgrades the expression of love? Got me analyzing things around with renewed perspective. Feeling all special and shit. Damn, God thought this much of me to put this person together that laughs at me knowing I ain't even that damn funny. A testament of God continually shining on me. Sending reminders with every giggle, kiss, and hug. Divine masculine, balanced within him own self so when I'm flying off the handle, he touches my arm and says, baby, relax. You don't have to figure it out in one day. Even when the roads become winding and the vision hazy, he stands in his power. Equivocally unafraid of his many facets. How can a man recognize me without surrendering to his own divinity? Loving himself forges the way to loving me. Catalyzing a multitude of changes in me. It's hard to describe but loving from a place of inspiration reduces the need to manipulate how the love is received. I can love him and still stand tall, still be me. I don't believe in capturing light, I believe a person draws beacons of experiences, breaking their expectations and expanding their humanity. Living authentically in a world that beats you down for being yourself. You're a fountain of individuality and magical wealth. How could I ever disrespect you? How could I ever abandon you? My forever muse. The one I'll make space for even when the world refuses your warmth, a true tested mirror. The one soliciting the nastiness in me. After wielding the staff of our divine offspring, you sensually kiss my lips help me up, and tap me on my ass saying that's my Queen. Will you ascend with me? Will abandoning our connection help understand the weight of loving you freely? Even in your release you're still the other whole of me. Forming the highest frequency of intimacy, honesty. For your truths I'm forever grateful.

Divine Masculine to Divine Feminine

And if I told you a thousand times how beautiful you are to me; would you believe it? Could you fully receive my admiration for you? Yes, God thinks highly of you, but She must really love me. Constructing so perfectly someone as caring, as bold, as silly as you. A woman that speaks to my soul with clarity and changes the energy of any room she walks into. No one knows the real power of a Goddess until they have met you. The freeness you emit scares many but not me. I realize freeness draws you nearer to me. You, my love, embody sacred synergy. Anointing my body with oil, frankincense and myrrh, bringing that Jesus energy. One look from those big eyes nourishes my spirit. This connection supersedes any coveting.

You reside in God's grace. How do you know when you love someone? I journeyed the garden of Eden and I can confirm it's not a place. Your granny said life was not a flower bed in Eden, that's because she couldn't experience something your mama had to give birth to. I met love when I recognized you. Why would you leave me? You speak to me in the sweetest tones. A voice of vibrational healing. Even while triggering you, you step up to the test. Instead of protecting wrongs, you ask what could be right? That's patience you swear you don't have. Ascending us into the next level of blessings and a myriad of new ways to love. Abandon me? Not when you've unchained my love. Celestial being, you think you walking away when my pussy feels that tight. My sunshine, dissolving every plight the world casts upon me. Even if I left, it would elevate us to a place where you would feel safer, more loved, more protected and freer showing your femininity. Divine feminine, no halves exist within this unity. You might not get everything you want but you're sure to get what you need. That's Source magnifying our divinity. For your love I'm forever grateful.

Thankfulness

I'm living in a way that honors my spirits and shows gratitude for my life. Feeling every part of my human enlightenment. I hope you find pieces of yourself in my words. As always may my growth provide guidance and encouragement.

Thank you for your energy

Asé to the Ancestors.

About The Author

Sade Hobson is the Chief Darling of Doohicky Craftique, LLC and resides in Mobile, AL. She's also an Amazon best-selling author of "Welcome Individuality: A Journey to Self-Love". She believes the world is its best place when people are empowered to define their personal power by living authentically. She embodies this lifestyle through holistic healing, helping others through her practice as a Reiki practitioner. She strives to live her life in a way that allows people to "Welcome their Individuality. "Sade has features on local television and national magazines for helping people actualize their individuality."

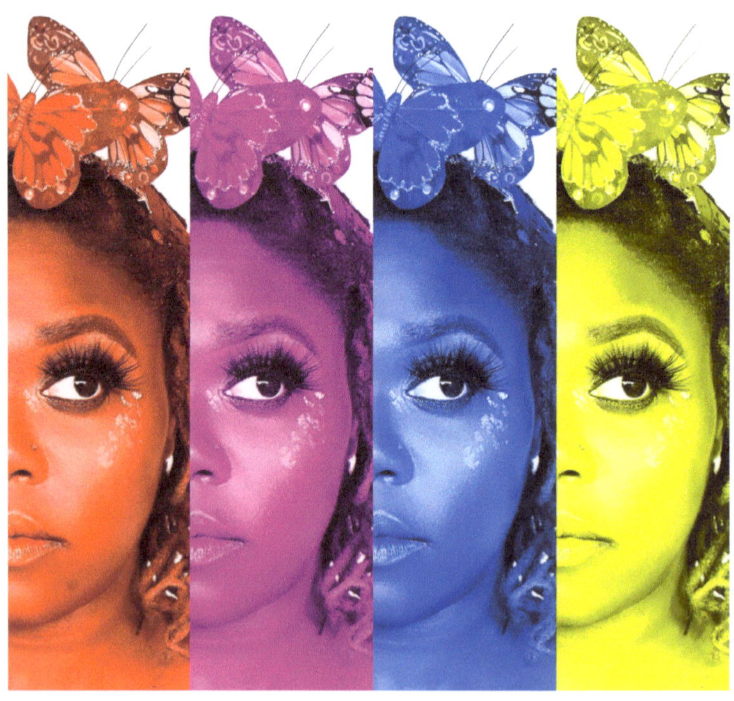

www.ingramcontent.com/pod-product-compliance
Lightning Source LLC
LaVergne TN
LVHW052255100826
845147LV00001B/48

* 9 7 8 1 7 3 4 8 6 1 5 2 5 *